LIVING
POSITIVELY
one day at a time

D0889478

by
Dr. Robert
Schuller

VOLUME 3 FOR '83!

Presented To

_____

By_____

Date_____

Introduction

Living positively, one day at a time has been a life-time adventure for me.

How often we are literally bombarded with the "noisy nuisances" of life: a loud bus and its fumes, a disagreeable boss, a traffic jam, or a fly in the soup!

And, too, our daily lives encounter the terrible tragedies such as the death of a loved one, the loss of a limb. A doctor's detection of a tumor. Or a divorce that threatens your home or the home of someone very close to you.

My life-time adventure with possibility thinking has certainly taught me one thing:

"Tough times never last...but tough people do!"

You can achieve, if you will believe, the words that are printed on the pages of this daily reader.

CONTENTS

JULY—POWER TO MAKE YOUR
    DREAMS COME TRUE
  Turn-Around Power
  Goal-Reaching Power
  Problem-Solving Power
  Achieving Power

AUGUST—TUNE INTO YOUR INNER POSSIBILITIES
  Possibilities—they are within you!
  Nothing is impossible
  Problems? Obstacles?—Nevertheless—It's possible!
  Dreaming makes it possible
  It's possible to keep your dream alive

SEPTEMBER—GET SET FOR A MIRACLE
  Believe in Miracles
  Expect a Miracle
  Count your miracles every day
  Turn your mountains into Miracles
  The one Miracle you'll never forget

OCTOBER—GOD'S WAY TO THE GOOD LIFE
  Commitment—The pathway to the good life
  Responsibility—The runway of "no turning back"
  Communication—The roadway to success
  Nourishment—The only way to make it all the way
  A positive Attitude—The gateway to the greatway

NOVEMBER—DISCOVER AN ENTHUSIASTIC
    NEW LIFE TODAY
  Live Right
  Love Right
  Think Right
  Give Right
  Pray Right

DECEMBER—LOOK TO THE MANGER
    TO FIND GOD'S GIFTS FOR YOU
  The gift of *Faith*
  The gift of *Love*
  The gift of *Joy*
  The gift of *Peace*
  The gift of *Hope*

REACH OUT FOR
A NEW LIFE

Try It

*"Seek first the kingdom of God, and His
righteousness; and all these things shall be
yours as well."*

Matthew 6:33

God has a dream for you in 1983 and He wants you to
grab hold of it. Your dream can come true if it passes five
simple principles. Try it. Eye it. Buy it. Fly it. Tie it down.
So reach out for a new life this year! Start right now by
giving it a try!

By that I mean, test it. Ask the question, is this God's
dream for my life? First, is it really needed? Does this bright
dream fill a vital human need? Does it help people who are
hurting? The secret of success is to find a need and fill it.
Can your dream really inspire? Can it be beautiful? Unless
it is beautiful it violates something deep in the human spirit.
Will your dream excel? Can you do it a little better and more
beautifully than anybody else? That's not an ego trip. What it
is is a devotion to a positive idea with a sense of reverence.

I am driven by an insatiable compulsion to excel. Here's
why: A positive idea that's God's idea deserves to be treated
like God deserves to be treated, without spot or wrinkle,
perfectly. Try it!

Close your eyes and ask God to give you a new dream
for a new year. Visualize it. Try it. Write it down.

_____

_____

_____

What dreams would you have if
you knew you could not fail?

Eye It

"Where there is no vision, the people perish."
                              Proverbs 29:18

Success stems from the fulfillment of a deep urge to help people who need to be helped.

I lectured a couple months ago at the School of Business Administration, University of California at Irvine. We had heads of the largest corporations in Southern California in my classroom, sixty of them. I asked them, "Where do goals rise from? Where do you get your dreams?" And I put it on the blackboard. Some goals rise out of the ego needs of the power structure. It's amazing how many businesses, how many institutions, how many individuals, establish their dreams and goals based on their unfulfilled ego needs. You can be sure that if the major goals rise out of the unfilled ego needs of the power structure, failure is inevitable because with the passing of time people will spot it, and nobody supports an ego tripper.

Go into prayer right now. Ask God to reveal to you the source of your dreams and goals for this new year. Ask Him to purify them and to make them as beautiful as He is. Then commit yourself to them and to Him.

When you find God's dream for your life, it is impossible to fail unless you decide you want to fail.

Eye It

"And you must think constantly about these commandments which I am giving you today. You must teach them to your children and talk about them when you are at home or out for a walk; at bedtime and the first thing in the morning. Tie them on your finger, wear them on your forehead, and write them on the doorposts of your house!"
Deuteronomy 6:6-9

Once your dream has passed the first test, eye it. Visualize it, write it down, draw a picture, put it on the board, stick it on your mirror, but get a picture. It is when you begin to see it in your mind that it becomes a fact. The other day I was reading Dr. Norman Vincent Peale's book *Positive Principles Today.* In it he says, "If you can visualize it and hold it for two years, it will come to pass." I believe this. The Crystal Cathedral is here today because we visualized it.

Decide right now some concrete ways that will help you visualize your new dream. Be creative. Start visualizing today!

I will see it because I believe it!

Eye It

"The most prominent among you must be as the youngest, and the leader as one who serves."
                                              Luke 22:26

Ask God what His plan is. Look at your situation and your dream through His eyes. Perhaps God's dream for you this year is for you to change your attitude toward your situation. Maybe you've been looking at it selfishly instead of from a service perspective. Perhaps God wants you just where you are in order to share God's love with others.

Maybe your job is not just a job; maybe it could be your ministry. It's very possible that Jesus would like to be working where you are, because the people around you need what Christ has to bring to them. You can be used by God to change your little part of the world. God has a better plan, and He's just waiting for you to ask and to pray so that He can show it to you.

God has a better plan!

Eye It

"The burning sand shall become a pool."
                                        Isaiah 35:7

The greatest discovery yet to be made is the discovery of the opportunities that you have in living—the undeveloped, non-actualized potential within you that waits to be discovered like a lost treasure. Look for it. When you find it, you can help make your dreams come true. A new life is waiting for you when you begin to make use of your hidden, God-given treasure.

Many of you are cynics. You once had dreams of a beautiful marriage, but it has turned to dust. You once dreamed of a successful business, but you went bankrupt. Your life is like a desert and the dreams are like mirages. You don't believe that there can be an oasis in the desert. You don't believe that there is treasure to be found. But you are wrong. Your mirage can become a pool, an actual oasis. Your dream *can* become a reality! That great idea *can* become a fact! That impossible, alluring hope *can* come true!

Keep looking! one of these times what looks like another mirage will become a pool, and you can drink and be fulfilled.

Eye It

"To open their eyes, that they may turn from darkness to light and from the power of Satan to God, that they may receive forgiveness of sins and a place among those who are sanctified by faith in Me."

Acts 26:18

Everything changes when you have the burst of new belief. The most beautiful experience in your life is when you come to have your eyes opened to the power of faith. The beautiful moment in life is when your eyes are opened and you see the face of Jesus. When you become a possibility thinker, you discover the potential of power within yourself. Then you receive the power to make your dreams come true. That's when you can really reach out for a new life. Why not make 1983 the year you really opened your eyes to God and the plans He has for you.

I believe God is going to do something in your life, and you'll see what you have not seen before and you will never forget it. Let God open your spiritual eyes, and you will see everything in life in a new and more beautiful way. You will dream new dreams, and God will help you make your dreams come true.

Open your eyes to new horizons.

Eye It

"But He said to me, 'My grace is sufficient for you, for my power is made perfect in weakness.' I will all the more gladly boast of my weaknesses, that the power of Christ may rest upon me."
II Corinthians 12:9

George W. Campbell was born blind. At the age of six, his mother sat down and took his little hands in hers. She counted his fingers and began, "George, people have five senses. Your thumb stands for hearing; you can hear me talk to you. Your index finger stands for touching; you can feel me touch you. Your next little finger stands for tasting. You can taste the food that you eat. Your fourth finger is for smelling; you can smell it when I bake bread. And your last little finger stands for seeing." Then she took that little finger and tied it to the palm of his hand with a rope.

"George," she said, "you're different from other boys. Your little finger doesn't work; you can't see. Right now you have four fingers, and I've got the fifth one tied down. Put out your hands; I'm going to throw a ball to you. Here it comes—catch it!" He caught it and she explained, "See George! As you grow up, remember that you can catch a ball even though you're missing one finger. You can catch hold of life and live a full and wonderful life even though you cannot see." And George became a positive, creative and fruitful person.

You can catch a ball even though you're missing one finger.

Eye It

"'Master,' his disciples asked Him, 'why was this man born blind? Was it a result of his own sins or those of his parents?' 'Neither,' Jesus answered. 'But to demonstrate the power of God'"

John 9:2-3

By the time George Campbell became a young man, a cure was discovered for congenital bilateral cataracts. He went through two surgeries on each eye, praying and hoping to see. When the bandages were at last removed, his doctor asked, "George, do you see anything?" He could only see what looked like a dull blur. Then he heard a voice over his face saying, "George, this is your mother. Can you see me?"

The blur became a color, the color took on a shape, and suddenly, for the first time in his life, he saw a human face. It belonged to a sixty-two year old woman and was wrinkled and framed with white hair. Later he was to say, "The most beautiful moment of my life was when my eyes were opened and I saw the beautiful face of my mother."

Open your eyes to the possibilities that God has locked up for you!

Buy It

"Commit everything you do to the Lord. Trust Him to help you do it and He will."

Psalm 37:5

If this is God's dream, and it is God's idea for your life, and you've tried it and eyed it, the third thing is to buy it. That means to make the commitment before you have solved the problem. Be totally sold on the idea. Be willing to pay the price.

I have been a dreamer for twenty-eight years. Every time we have moved ahead to do something great for God—our Neutra sanctuary, the Tower of Hope, the Crystal Cathedral, the Hour of Power—at every point I was so convinced that it was God's idea that I would have gladly died for the success of the dream.

Nothing can stop a person who:
1. knows this is God's dream
2. knows if he drops the ball, he will be committing sacrilege against his Lord by spoiling one of the ideas He gave like a jewel into his stewardship.

Make the commitment before you have solved the problems.

Buy It

"Again, the kingdom of heaven is like a merchant in search of fine pearls, who, on finding one pearl of great value, went and sold all that he had and bought it."

Matthew 13:46

Believe in the big, beautiful idea that unfolds into your mind. It will seem impossible—God's ideas are always impossible when they first strike us. If there were no obstacles, no problems, no risk of failure, it wouldn't require belief at all—and the idea might not really have come from God. God wants to stretch us, to help us grow! Belief is only exercising faith and faith is taking a chance on something you can't prove.

Commit yourself to God's ideas when they come. Commit yourself to begin to work on them. Commit yourself to continue to work on them. A new life is waiting for you just beyond the horizon!

Faith is taking a chance on something you can't prove.

Buy It

"Jesus told him, 'No one who puts his hand to the plow and looks back is fit for the kingdom of God.'"

Luke 9:62

I am a runner, but there are some mornings when I really don't feel like running. Arvella and I take extended trips in the summers, ministering to people around the world, and often it is difficult to keep up a running schedule. It takes a tremendous amount of discipline and commitment.

I'll never forget one morning in Lucerne, Switzerland. I woke up and said to myself, "I'm too lazy to run today." But I forced myself to get out and get going. Along the lake, I saw a man hobbling along on two crutches, one of his legs having been amputated at the knee. He looked at me hungrily, his eyes pleading, "Oh God, I wish I could run!"

I came to a bridge, and an elderly woman was pushing her husband in a wheelchair. He had no legs at all, and he had that same look—like a starving child looking through the window at a fat man feasting on food. He craned his head to look back at me as I sped away on my two good legs.

I ran four miles that day, and I never missed running a single day in all my hopping around planet earth that summer!

Be committed–go the extra mile!

Buy It

"Have two goals: wisdom—that is, knowing and doing right—and common sense. Don't let them slip away, for they fill you with living energy, and are a feather in your cap."

                                        Proverbs 3:21-22

When he reached the North Pole, Captain Scott wrote bitterly in his diary, "Goodbye to our daydreams." I'm afraid that you also may be tempted to say the same. "I tried God and it didn't work. I tried to remain morally clean, but I fell again. I tried to stay with my resolutions, but I broke them. I tried to live up to my youthful ideals, but I saw everyone shattering theirs and having fun, so I decided to do likewise. Life is too short to waste it on daydreams. I'm going to grab what I can when I can and believe only what I can taste, eat, drink and feel."

This is a call to choose—to be either young all your days or to decide now to become old. People who never lose faith in buried treasures are like little children. People who keep dreaming dreams remain perpetually young. But people who are not committed to their dreams and their ideals and their faith become cynical and give up their youthful ideals. That is when and how they become old.

I hereby commit myself to my God and my dreams and I shall never really grow old.

Buy It

". . . But the righteous shall live by his faith."
Habakkuk 2:4

My challenge to you today is to do something—make a commitment—that will challenge your faith. Faith only grows when you do something to challenge it. It's like muscles in the body. They will get weak and flabby unless you continue to exercise them to the point where upon occasion you can feel pain. That's a fundamental truth and principle.

The tragedy is that there are so many people who have no happiness. Because they have no happiness, they have no self confidence. Because they have no self confidence, they don't dare try anything new. Because they won't try anything new, they just get weaker. That makes their self confidence decline until it's old, weak, flabby and useless. The only way to build faith and self confidence is to challenge it!

There is no gain without pain.

Buy It

"I will be found by you, and I will end your slavery and restore your fortunes."

Perhaps in your dreams for a new life, you are struggling against habits. What are they? Smoking? Drinking? Narcotics? Commit yourself to God and your dream, and He will help you to snap the trap. He makes that promise to you.

Mrs. Schuller and I attended the International Congress of Psychologists in Paris, France where we went to a specialized workshop on Behavioral Modification. That is the attempt to take someone who has an established behavior pattern and try to alter it permanently. The chairman of the event was discouraged before he even began. "How can we bring about behavior modification in our patients when we are not in control of our own behavior?" he lamented. "We probably all smoke, drink, and eat too much and exercise too little."

I can declare to you with total conviction, there is no psychologist, no psychiatrist, no therapy in the world that can change human behavior like the Gospel of Jesus Christ and the power of God!

**Commit yourself—
and God will snap the trap!**

Buy It

"Lord, you alone can heal me, you alone can save, and my praises are for you alone."
                                        Jeremiah 17:14

God's got a plan. Believe you can do it, even though you've never done anything like it in your life. Make a commitment, because belief always calls for commitment, and commitment always leads to discipline. Then, expect a miracle! There will be a breakthrough when suddenly you know you're on top of it. The trap is snapped! You've been set free. Jesus Christ has helped you to reach out for a new life, achieve your goals, put down cigarettes, drinking, narcotics, depression, or despair. You'll look back and see it's like being converted. And maybe that's exactly what happened. Maybe you had never been converted before. You are born again! Praise God!

Belief always calls for commitment.

Fly It

*"If anyone publicly acknowledges Me as his friend,
I will openly acknowledge him as my friend before
my Father in heaven."*

Matthew 10:32

Fly it! This simply means to begin. Like a little
boy with a kite, start running and see if it can catch
the wind, and before you know it, the positive idea
is out. People will come to your support that you
would never have dreamed of. The Crystal
Cathedral shimmers in the sun, proclaiming to the
world the love of God, and it was built by people
across the United States who were excited and
gave generously. Positive ideas attract support
from the most unexpected sources!

So promise yourself to make a start today; begin
to tell others about your dream. Share the ideas
you have for an exciting new life that will be
fulfilling to you and others too. You hold the bell
in your hand. It remains for you to lift it high and
begin to ring it so its clear, beautiful tones can
show God's love to a hurting world.

A bell is no bell until you ring it.

Fly It

"But Jesus said, 'Let the little children come to Me, and don't prevent them. For such is the Kingdom of Heaven.'"

Mark 10:14

Norm Rasmussen operated the sound system for the church. He and his wife had four children, all sons. When Sarah became pregnant again, they prayed for a girl, and God gave them a girl. Leah. She was born with Down's Syndrome, permanently mentally retarded. It was a tragic blow, but her parents decided to turn their problem into a project. They took on more mongoloid and retarded children as foster parents. God gave them His love for these children.

When Norm lost his job, they once again turned their problem into an opportunity, and moved into the country, building a large home there. Norm and Sarah now have over thirty brain damaged or mentally limited children that they care for and love. They had a problem—a big one—but instead of sinking under its weight, they flew it over the horizon into a new life.

Turn your problems into projects.

Fly It

"Be strong! Be courageous! Do not be afraid of them! For the Lord your God will be with you. He will neither fail you nor forsake you."

Deuteronomy 31:6

As you begin to fly your dream, remember that as soon as a positive idea enters the mind, negative thoughts, like nipping dogs, come to scare the positive idea away. Be on guard against the little dogs of fear that will come nipping at you in the form of negative reactions to this great idea. You must exercise courage to move out and be the success God wants you to be. Then you'll end up with a by-product called Self-Confidence. And boy, you can't put a price tag on that!

**Self confidence cannot be taught,
it has to be caught!**

Fly It

"Remember, your Father knows exactly what you need even before you ask Him!"
Matthew 6:8

When our first children were babies, we were just establishing our church here, and most of the time we were flat broke. We had times when there was no food on the table or milk for the babies. One particular occasion, we were tempted to take the five dollar bill out of the offering envelope and use it for milk. We have always given ten percent of our income to God, though, and we knew we couldn't use that money. It wasn't really ours, so we trusted God.

I found some postage stamps and tried to get the post office to redeem them for cash. They wouldn't. Then I tried to get the market to trade me some milk for them. They wouldn't. Then the mail came, and I'll never forget it. In the mail was a five dollar bill from my mother!

**Make a start, trusting God—
He'll see you through.**

Fly It

"Try it! let me prove it to you! If you do, I will open up the windows of heaven for you and pour out a blessing so great you won't have room enough to take it in!"

Malachi 3:10

I walked around our grounds recently, and let me share with you what a ministry God has given us. Over ten thousand ministers and church leaders from around the world have been trained in our Institute for Successful Church Leadership. Today, millions are a part of our Hour of Power television ministry. Through New Hope counseling, we are preventing an average of more than two suicides a week.

You'd be thrilled on a Wednesday or Thursday night to find our Youth Center jammed with one thousand high school kids, half of them having been brought by their friends who are Christians. We are saving so many kids from dope, and God knows what. We reach so far. What God can do with what you give to Him is unbelievable.

God can do more with us and our resources than we can by keeping them in our own hands.

Fly It

"Blessed is the man who trusts in the Lord, whose trust is in the Lord."

Jeremiah 17:7

I was in college when I made the decision to give God ten per cent of my income. It wasn't much; I just worked at menial tasks like cleaning toilets and washing dishes to earn my way through school. It was one of the most impossible decisions I have ever made in my life. Have you just made an impossible decision? Do you feel trapped? I did. Here is what God told me.

"You can trust me, Schuller. You need faith for the life that I have planned for you, powerful faith, and the only way to get it is to stick your neck out and do something beautiful that's impossible, to give me a chance to prove that I do take care of my own."

**Put yourself in God's hands—
He takes care of His own.**

Fly It

"Your right hand, oh Lord, is glorious in power...."
Exodus 15:6

A group of women who lived on the bayou in Louisiana were complaining one day because they didn't live in the city and didn't have luxurious homes. One of the women was a positive thinker. She got so tired of the complainers and faultfinders that she finally looked at them and said, "Look, you live on the bayou. The bayou flows into the ocean. You've got a boat. You can go anywhere from where you are!"

When you begin to believe in God, it's like having a house on the bayou. Because God, like the bayou, has the power to take you to where you want to go. There is no end to God's power and God's possibilities to do something within you. And when you touch faith with God, you can go anywhere. Your faith is the boat. You have to take action. Your boat has a motor, but you have to start it.

You can go anywhere from where you are with the power of God.

Tie It Down

"In all toil there is profit, but mere talk tends only to want."

Proverbs 14:23

Don't quit. Dreams have an enormous inclination to want to drift away when frustration and despair move in and discouragement comes. Try it; test your dream out. Eye it; visualize it. Buy it; make the commitment. Fly it; move out in faith. And tie it down and you have the power to make your dreams come true and open up a brand new life for 1983.

When it's all said and done, the only way to bring a dream into a concrete reality is to never give up until it has been accomplished.

I won't give up! I won't give up! Say those positive words over and over to yourself. Make yourself and your God a promise.

I promise not to give up!

Tie It Down

"The Lord will be the hope of His people and the strength of the children of Israel."

Joel 3:16

Stanley Reimer was an elder in the church for many years. One day he suffered a twenty minute cardiac arrest; by the time he got to the hospital, he was comatose. His neurologist said that for his brain to go without oxygen and nutrients for such an extended period that there would be no possibility of life, to say nothing of recovery!

But I believe what Dr. Smiley Blanton once said, "There are vast undamaged areas in the most damaged brain." When I went to visit Stan in the hospital, I assumed he could hear. "Stanley," I said, "this is Dr. Schuller. You're going to get well." A tear rolled out of his eye and trickled down his cheek. It was the first sign of hope.

Stanley got a dream in his comatose condition, a dream that he could recover. And he didn't give up hope. Stanley has made a fantastic recovery. God is great! He won't let your dream come smashing down!

Keep on keeping on.

Tie It Down

"Commit your work to the Lord, and your plans will be established."

Proverbs 16:3

I was only five years old when I decided I wanted to become a preacher. When I realized all the education it would entail and the great cost of it, I nearly despaired. We were poor farmers during the dustbowl in Iowa. But I kept hoping.

One day at the age of twelve, I went with my dad into the First National Bank of Orange City, Iowa. I stood there, feeling out of place in my patched overalls, but a calendar on the wall caught my eye. There was a slogan on that calendar, and I read it and memorized it. It changed my life.

It read, "Great people are ordinary people with an extra amount of determination".

How great I become is determined by the degree of my determination.

Tie It Down

"To everyone who overcomes—who to the very end keeps on doing things that please me—I will give power over the nations."

Revelation 2:26

Money doesn't matter, prestige doesn't matter, connections don't matter. Determination is everything. I will not quit! If you could reach into the inner hearts of great men and women, I can tell you what you will find. At the heart of every great person and at the heart of every great movement there is a veil. Draw the veil and you will see a little golden door. Unlock that door and out of the door will fall four words, I WILL NOT QUIT!

Great people are common people committed to uncommon goals.

Tie It Down

"Fear not, for I have redeemed you; I have called you by name, you are mine."

Isaiah 43:1

Once God had a big beautiful idea. He decided to create a world and turn it into a garden and create people in His own image. That meant people who could think and make decisions and who could say yes or no. People who had an active imagination, a sense of humor and a nature that would compel them to love and give. He packaged the whole thing so the world was finished and the garden complete. And He put man and woman in it.

Then everything fell apart. His dream got a crack in it and fell to pieces. His children, who were to have been His friends, were hiding in the bushes because of their guilt. The Lord looked down from His throne in heaven and I dare to believe that he thought four words, "I will not quit!".

God has a big, beautiful ideal for you.

Tie It Down

"And Christ became a human being and lived here on earth among us and was full of loving forgiveness and truth. And some of us have seen His glory—the glory of the only Son of the Heavenly Father!"

John 1:14

God's patience is eternal. He sent the prophets and they were stoned. He sent His spokesmen and they were killed. Finally He said, "I will come down to this world and I will look like a man, and I will be like every other man except that I will not sin."

And so He came. He called Himself Jesus Christ, the Son of God. And the world has never been the same since. I don't care if you're an atheist or an anti-Christian, you have to admit I'm right. The world is still not perfect, but the world is not the same place it was before Jesus entered it.

Patience say "I will not quit!"

Tie It Down

"The Lord God has given us this land. Go and possess it as he told us to. Don't be afraid! Don't even doubt!"

Deuteronomy 1:21

I will not quit! I say to you that these four words are God's antidote to man's biggest emotional problem. Discouragement.

There's a legend that says that one day Satan and his cohorts were commiserating together about the rise of Christianity in the world. "We've got a big problem," Satan said, "Jesus makes a big difference in the life of every believer, and together they are doing too much good for the world. I don't like it."

The other devils agreed and began to discuss ways that they might counteract this problem. They decided against lust, because Christians have true love for each other and wouldn't settle for second best. They rejected love of money, because they reasoned that the Christians would just go out and make more so they could give more away.

Finally one little devil came up with an ingenious idea. "Let's fill them up with discouragement! We'll get them to looking at all the unsaved people in the world, we'll help them to concentrate on the sins and evils of the world until they are so discouraged that they'll become cynical. Then they won't believe in hope any more, and that will lead to feelings of despair. Once they're despairing, they'll be defeated."

Don't be discouraged—never give up hope.

Tie It Down

"This man came to Jesus by night, and said to him, 'Rabbi, we know that you are a teacher sent by God: for no man can do these miracles that you do, unless God is with him.'"

John 3:2

I have an Hour of Power viewer in Illinois who was the beauty queen of her high school at the age of nineteen when she suffered a tragic accident. The homecoming queen found herself in a coma with no hope. After four months, her doctor suggested to her mother that they remove the intravenous feeding tubes and let her starve to death. After all, she was already shriveled up to a mere sixty-five pounds, twisted in grotesque proportions. But her mother had faith in God and refused to give up hope.

Today she is thirty-six years old and almost normal with only a slight limp and a slight speech impediment. She is married and has a beautiful child of her own. She says, "I believe in miracles." So do I!

**Faith and hope believe in miracles—
that's why they never give up.**

Tie It Down

"....Through two unchangeable things, in which it is impossible that God should prove false, we who have fled for refuge might have strong encouragement to seize the hope set before us."
Hebrews 6:18

Never stop believing in hope. God never promised He would give you what you wanted or what you asked for when you ask for it. You can look all through your Bible and collect all the promises of God, but there isn't a single one that says He will give you what you want when you want it. If He did, it would probably create problems for someone else. Or maybe it would keep you from maturing in your faith, or maybe even He has something better in mind for you than what you asked for.

God's delays are not God's denials. You must be patient year after year. He is at work. He has a plan. Keep on believing in hope.

**Lord, I'll never give up my quest
to be great for Your glory.**

LOVE IS THE GREATEST

Love Dissolves Loneliness

".....Yet I will not be alone, for the Father is with me."

John 16:32

It is impossible for you or any human being to saturate your mind and soul with the teachings of I Corinthians 13 and not have a life-renewing experience. I say that because in dealing with the greatest subject, it closes with ".....and the greatest is love."

Notice it does not say, "...and the greatest is religion." It's not enough to have religion. There is no substitute for true love.

There's a loneliness in wrestling with all of the potential solutions to problems that block your path. You can talk to some, but if you really want to know how lonely a person is, all you need do is overhear their most intimate prayers. You'd find that many people are really searching for solutions, struggling up that mountain in life. Who among us dares to admit that we need help? Those words are hard to say.

You can see what's wrong. The paradox of loneliness is pride, destructive pride which is the absence of deep inner security. Only the self confident person dares to admit that he doesn't know it all and needs help.

Your deepest need is the awareness that you are not really alone in life's lonely moments.

Love Dissolves Loneliness

"But we by the help of the Holy Spirit are counting on Christ's death to clear away our sins and make us right with God."

Galatians 5:5

Sin brings with it a heartbreaking loneliness, the terrible loneliness of not being able to admit to anybody what your secret sins are. Some of you are suffering from the torturing loneliness of carrying in your mind the secret of some sin you are in the process of committing or planning or a recent sin still fresh in your memory. Who do you share it with?

Enter Jesus Christ. Jesus Christ has a cure for loneliness, for through Him real love truly comes into our lives! And He is the one friend that we can all count on and believe in.

Jesus brings true love into our lives.

Love Dissolves Loneliness

*"Come to me, all who labor and are heavy laden,
and I will give you rest."*
                              Matthew 11:28

Only people who know how to love can be
lonely. For loneliness is a desperate hunger to fulfill
a need for fellowship with someone to whom we
can share our deepest secrets without the fear of
being rejected. That is why machines will never
get lonely. And loneliness is proof that you need
God.

You must take that last lonely step and
surrender your mind, your logic, as well as your
emotional structure. Surrender your logic to love!
In the final analysis, not to surrender your logic to
love is the ultimate illogical decision!

Surrender your mind, yourself, to God, to Jesus
Christ! For God did come to visit this earth. He
did die on a cross; that's a fact. I believe He rose
again on Easter and that He is alive this very
moment!

Surrender your logic to God's love.

Love Dissolves Loneliness

"And now He has made all of this plain to us by the coming of our Saviour Jesus Christ, who broke the power of death and showed us the way of everlasting life through trusting Him."
II Timothy 1:10

I've been lonely and circling, trying to make decisions. I have been lonely in striving and in searching for solutions. I have been lonely in struggling to reach the top of the mountain, and I have been lonely in sinking and lonely in sinning. But through it all, the loneliness was healed by the one intimate close friend, Jesus. And someday I shall step out of this earth, all alone, into eternity. My soul will leave my body, and when that happens, I will not really walk alone. My Jesus and my God will be with me.

That's what salvation is! I offer it to you now. That kind of faith; it's not an argument at all—it's a decision! It's not a debate. I won't debate you 1 about it. It is a decision! And it's not an intellectual conflict. It is a commitment!

Thank you, Jesus, for healing my loneliness.

Love Dissolves Loneliness

"And He has showered down upon us the richness of His grace—for how well He understands us and knows what is best for us at all times."
Ephesians 1:8

Why are people lonely? Because they lack the courage to love, that's why. To love so deeply that you run the risk of being hurt. You know, people choose loneliness over the fear of being disappointed and really hurt. And that is not a good trade! Not when you can choose to love Jesus Christ and know that He loves you because He'll never, never hurt you.

Pray this prayer with me:
Thank you Lord, that we don't ever have to be lonely again. Thank you Lord, that there is peace that is surrounding us now. It is the presence of the Christ who lived, who died, who has transcended and who transcends body and time and space and lives in that dimension that makes it possible for Him to communicate with us and we with Him. Thank you Jesus Christ, for the faith that is being born in us now. You are that wonderful friend. We love you. Thank you for loving us. Amen.

I don't ever have to be lonely again, because Jesus is my friend.

Love Solves Problems

"For God so loved the world that He gave His only Son, that whoever believes in Him should not perish but have eternal life."

John 3:16

Love is not the easiest. It can be very difficult. Love is not the cheapest. It can be terribly costly. (God's love cost Him His Son on the cross.) It's not the safest way to live. In fact, it's down-right risky.

Every time you allow yourself to become emotionally involved, you put yourself in a very vulnerable position. Whether it's an idea, a dream, or a relationship, it's going to be costly in the long run. It's not going to be cheap. The Bible says love may not be the cheapest, it may not be the easiest, it may not be the safest way to live, but love is the greatest!

Love is costly—but well worth the price.

Love Solves Problems

".....And the prophet replied, 'the Lord is able to give you much more than this!'"
                                II Corinthians 25:9

Love is the greatest because it's available to every person. No person is too small for God's love. No problem is too big for God's power.

The other day I entered the Cathedral with Bob Jani and pointed out to him that the entrance to this Cathedral has the lowest ceiling of any chapel or church in the United States. The ceiling in my home is eight feet, six inches. I cannot touch it with my fingertips. But the ceilings under the balconies of the Cathedral are so low that I can lay my hands flat on the ceiling. So, it is thrilling to step from under the low balconies into the awesome expanse of the main sanctuary. It's like a reminder that nobody is too small to touch God. And no problem is too big for His power.

No problem is too big for God's power.

Love Solves Problems

"But God is so rich in mercy; He loved us so much that even though we were spiritually dead and doomed by our sins, He gave us back our lives again when He raised Christ from the dead—only by His undeserved favor have we ever been saved."

Ephesians 2:4-5

God has set up this world so that the littlest person can get his food. Some people are super-rich, affluent and very well off while some people live very precariously from coin to coin and dollar to dollar. But when it comes to the greatest thing—love, God dishes it out so anybody can have their share. And if you've got love, you've got the greatest thing in the world. Love is the greatest, because it's available to all.

Thank you, God, for making your love available to all.

Love Solves Problems

"Most important of all, continue to show deep love for each other, for love makes up for many of your faults."

I Peter 4:8

Love is the greatest because it's the positive solution to any problem you have. Every problem is, ultimately, a lack of faith. Without love, faith loses its power.

Are you lonely? Bored? Do you have problems in interpersonal relationships? Are you offended? Tempted? Whatever it is—love offers a positive solution.

Without love, faith loses its power.

Love Solves Problems

".....for all we need is faith working through love."
Galatians 5:6

The positive solution to loneliness, boredom, promiscuity, racism, social injustice or any sin you can imagine, is not to be against them, but to plant something else so powerful that it consumes the problem. Love is that satisfying! It lifts you beyond temptations. Once you've enjoyed good music, you won't be interested in any other kind. If you are happily married and have a beautiful love in Christ, pornography isn't tempting.

Love is the greatest because it is the answer to every sin you can imagine, the positive solution to every problem.

**Love is the positive answer
to my every problem.**

Love Solves Problems

"This is what I have asked God for you: that you will be encouraged and knit together by strong ties of love, and that you will have the rich experience of knowing Christ with real certainty and clear understanding. For God's secret plan, now at last made known, is Christ Himself."

Colossians 2:2

Love is the greatest because it's the only thing that you cannot give away without having it come back to you again.

Recently I donated my Good Shepherd medallion to our charity auction. A lady in New York City who has watched Hour of Power faithfully, heard what was going to happen and decided she would buy the medallion regardless of the cost. She flew to California to attend the auction and was prepared to bid any amount. Value-wise it was worth only $1,000 in used gold, but she bought it for $6,400. All of the money went to our mission project.

The day after the auction, she stopped to see me before her return to New York. Enthusiastically, she said, "Dr. Schuller, the real reason I bought the medallion was because I felt you should always have it." At that point, she gave me back my medallion as a gift!

**Give love away and it multiplies
and comes back to you.**

Love Solves Problems

"For you are bought with a price: therefore glorify God in your body, and in your spirit, which are God's."

I Corinthians 6:20

I wear my Good Shepherd Medallion as a symbol of my life. First I liked it because somebody made it for me. Now I like it because, not only was it given once, but a second precious price was paid for it.

Do you know what? It's like your soul. First, God made it; then, Christ died for it. He paid a precious price to give life back to you. Jesus Christ fills you with love. Love isn't love until you give it away. Because when you give it away, only then does it come back. Love is the greatest! It is available to all. It solves all the problems. And it comes back in a beautiful way!

Love isn't love until you give it away.

Love Absolves Faith from Selfishness

"Your eyes are to see with—why don't you look? Why don't you open your ears and listen? Don't you remember anything at all?"

Mark 8:18

I am reminded of the story of the two old Dutchmen, sitting on a parkbench. The night had come and the moon had started to shine. Not far from the bench where they sat, a river flowed, and from the river came the chorus of the crickets. Pete, the first gentleman, listened to the crickets and said, "Crickets sure do like to sing." John, sitting next to him agreed, saying, "Yep, they sure know how to sing."

Just then he heard the voices of the choir coming from a nearby church and remarked, "Beautiful music, isn't it?" Pete said, "Yeah, and to think they do it just by rubbing their legs together."

Each heard a different music—one was listening to the crickets. The other heard the choir. Life is like that. God gave us senses with which to perceive our world, and yet our perception of any given situation depends on where we stand personally. Do you see and hear everything filtered through the love of God? When you do, your life is full of beauty.

What you hear depends on where you're coming from and where you're going.

Love Absolves Faith from Selfishness

"There are three things that remain—faith, hope, and love—and the greatest of these is love.
I Corinthians 13:13

"And now abides faith, hope, love, and the greatest of these is love."

I used to think this verse meant St. Paul was having a beauty contest and there were three lovelies who entered. The first was "Faith", the second "Hope", and the third "Love". The contest was held and "Love" won. "Faith" was number two and "Hope" was runner up.

Actually, what Paul is saying is that faith, hope and love make up the Holy Trinity which all of us can understand and believe in. Love is the ribbon that ties it all together. Love is what makes hope beautiful and faith reliable. Listen to these words from I Corinthians 13: "Love believes all things."

There is a terribly important relationship between love and faith. It is held in two significant sentences: Love without faith is impossible. And faith without love is totally unacceptable.

Faith without love is unacceptable.

Love Absolves Faith from Selfishness

"Love does no wrong to anyone. That's why it fully satisfies all of God's requirements. It is the only law you need."

Romans 13:10

Love puts power into faith! First, love puts a redeeming power into faith. Have you ever known someone who demonstrated great possibility thinking? Real positive thinking can move mountains. But unless faith is redeemed by love, faith can be not only unacceptable but downright demonic.

The Communists have mountain moving faith. The ungodly secularists have mountain moving faith. Mountain moving faith without the love of Jesus Christ is unacceptable. It's downright dangerous. There are people with a faith so strong that they can climb to the top, and they do; but unless their faith is controlled and wrapped by love, they hurt a lot of people on the way. Love makes faith redeemable. Without love, faith is hardly to be trusted.

Make sure your faith is controlled by love.

Love Absolves Faith from Selfishness

".....You shall love your neighbor as yourself."
Matthew 19:19

Without love, real faith in God is impossible. Why is it that there are people who can't believe in God? Why? Because they haven't seen God's love in action applied to them at a time when they were hurting. I've yet to see a person converted to a beautiful Christian faith except through the transmission experience of non-judgmental, unconditional, respecting love.

Without love, real faith in God is impossible.

Love Absolves Faith from Selfishness

"This is my command, that you love one another as I have loved you."

John 15:12

Mother Theresa founded "The Home of the Dying" in Calcutta, India. She is a beautiful Roman Catholic nun who left the convent with only five pennies and no knowledge of where her own food was coming from. She felt called by God to do one thing—to take people who were dying every day in the gutters and sidewalks of Calcutta and just love them.

Mother Theresa said, "The thing that saddens me as I walk through the streets is not the fact that people are dying, but that they're dying and nobody cares. They die and people walk over the bodies. Everyone deserves to die with dignity."

She's been asked many times where she gets the love to love the unlovely. Her answer is always the same. "From Jesus."

Jesus shows us how to love unconditionally.

Love Absolves Faith from Selfishness

"Now you can have real love for everyone because your souls have been cleansed from selfishness and hatred when you trusted Christ to save you; so see to it that you really do love each other warmly, with all your hearts."

I Peter 1:22

Love gives faith in God and Jesus Christ. If you don't believe in God, it's not your fault. It's mine. Somehow I have failed to show you the love of Jesus Christ. If you are not a believer in God, I have failed.

Give me and others a chance. Come close; do not run away. Give us a chance to show you true love. Love believes all things. Love puts real power into faith. Love will give you faith now.

Love believes all things.

Love Absolves Faith from Selfishness

"Yet it is always new, and works for you just as it did for Christ; and as we obey this commandment, to love one another, the darkness in our lives disappears and the new light of life in Christ shines in."

I John 2:8

If you can't find faith, or haven't experienced love from those around you, there is one way. Draw close to Jesus. Close your eyes. Invision a black ceiling; see the dungeon of despair. See a window appearing. It is the light of Jesus Christ. Look for heaven above. It is God. Let light flow into your mind. Let love flow into your heart. Let Jesus Christ come into your life.

As you do—the light that is in you will be forever greater than the darkness around you. Love will put faith in your life and power in your faith. Love without faith is impossible. Faith without love is unacceptable. Put them both together, and what a life you'll have!

**For a wonderful life—
let love and faith control you.**

Love Resolves Discord

"Finally, all of you, have unity of spirit, sympathy, love of the brethren, a tender heart and a humble mind."

I Peter 3:8

Inevitably our relationship with God through Christ releases real love within us. There is authentic love which is very healing as a positive emotion, and there is counterfeit love which is very destructive. What is the difference between the two? For instance, you've seen evidences of destructive love in marriages, between parent and child, between employer and employee, and between labor and management. On the other side of the coin, you've seen illustrations of healing, redeeming love. Real redeeming love is totally healing.

Authentic love is a positive emotion.

Love Resolves Discord

"May God who gives patience, steadiness, and encouragement help you to live in complete harmony with each other—each with the attitude of Christ toward the other."

Romans 15:5

Compromise is learning to let go. If you forget everything else, remember this: No person has a right to demand all his rights all the time. If you're abused, shocked or treated rudely, discourteously or unkindly—look beyond. Learn to let go. Let go of resentment, let go of jealousy, let go of the greed, fear, bitterness, hatred and hurt!

Real love doesn't demand its own way. It knows how to let go and latch on. Latch on to something that's tied down to something. What's the use of holding on to something that isn't tied down to anything? What is your "god"? Is it status? Fame? Money? What are you really after in life? Is it tied down?

**No person has the right to demand
all his rights all the time.**

Love Resolves Discord

"Beloved ones, if God loved us so much, we ought to love one another also. No one has ever seen God. If we love one another, God remains in us and His love has been perfected in us."
I John 4:12-13

There can be no community without com-promise. Love compromises. Love does not demand its own way. The difference between healing and sickness is salvation. Self condemna-tion can hinder that one word—compromise. You've met people with hardened options, iron wills, frozen viewpoints—they only produce sickness within themselves until they learn the warm quality of compromising.

Many Christians have been taught that com-promise is a dirty word. That's because classical Christianity has made little effort to distinguish between positive and negative thinking. Take the word compromise. There is such a thing as a negative compromise. When you compromise your ideals, your morals, your dreams, and your lofty goals; then, indeed, compromise becomes a negative word. But positive compromise is something else. There is no rising up the ladder intellectually, emotionally, socially, professionally, or spiritually, without discovering the power of compromise.

Love makes compromise a positive word.

Love Resolves Discord

"But he that is greatest among you shall be your servant."

Matthew 23:11

Positive compromise is lowering yourself. In other words, you are willing to surrender some of your own ideas and hardened opinions. Albert Schweitzer built a hospital in the jungles. One day he asked one of the natives to carry some wood. The native had been learning to read and write and replied, "I'd like to, sir, but it's beneath my dignity. I am a scholar—an intellectual."

Albert Schweitzer chuckled and said, "I've always wanted to be an intellectual too, but never quite made it, so I'll carry the wood!" And he went out and carried the wood.

God will help me to be willing to surrender my pride.

Love Resolves Discord

"And He sat down and called the twelve; and he said to them, 'If any one would be first, he must be last of all and servant of all.'"

Mark 9:35

I am reminded of Jesus and the disciples. The disciples were arguing about who was the best among them and who would be in command if Jesus left. Jesus watched this ego-tripping, opinionated conversation and said nothing. Instead, He took a bowl of water, stooped down and began to wash their feet. Peter protested and said, "Wait a minute, Lord. You can't wash my feet; I should wash yours." Jesus brushed him aside and continued washing the feet of His disciples. He wanted to teach them that if you want to climb, you have to come down first. If you want to learn, you have to admit you don't have all the answers. If you want to succeed more often, you have to listen to the problems and the criticisms that others have.

If you want to climb, first you must be willing to come down.

Love Resolves Discord

"Brothers, I do not imply that I have made it on my own, but one thing I do—forgetting what is behind and reaching out for what lies ahead, I push on to the goal for the high prize of God's heavenly call in Christ Jesus."
Philippians 3:13-14

Compromising is looking beyond the present moment to the big picture. You may have to compromise your feelings because of a tension or a problem in your marriage or relationships. Maybe there is a tension between you and God. Perhaps God didn't give you what you asked for. Maybe you feel He didn't answer your prayer and so you are angry. Maybe there is tension between you and your boss. If there is, probably you have to practice what I call looking at the big picture. In other words, compromise your feelings, your hurts, your rejections, and your despair. Forget about them.

Look at the big picture.

Love Resolves Discord

"Reverence of the Lord is the instruction of wisdom, for before honor must be humility."
                                        Proverbs 15:33

Compromise. It's another word for humility. Compromise looks at the big picture, swallows a lot of pride and absorbs a lot of hurt. Compromise is lowering yourself, looking beyond and listening. Listen to people who are smarter than you are. This is something I learned years ago. No matter what the subject, there is somebody who knows more about it than you do and you can learn from them.

The other day I spoke with a person who is living a very fast life. So fast that he doesn't have time to smell the flowers or touch the face of a child. His value system is all mixed up. I said to him, "What is the use of running so fast when you're on the wrong road?"

Take time to smell the flowers.

Love Revolves Around Others

"The charitable soul will be enriched, and he who waters, will himself be watered."

Proverbs 11:25

The most powerful motivating force in the world today is the love of God in our lives. The real secret of motivation is to fall in love with Love and fall in love with Life. Fall in love with living and you'll fall in love with giving. Your entire being will change! If your life seems bleak and barren and lacking in enthusiasm today, this is the answer for you. It's like the desert here in Southern California in the summer—nothing but sand, colorless and drab. But after the winter rains, an amazing thing happens. The bleak, barren sand begins to bloom into acres of blue and purple and red desert flowers. The seeds were always there, waiting for the right rains to fall and bring them to life. The same is true of you today; the seeds of your life are waiting to bloom.

**Fall in love with love and awaken
the beautiful flowers of your life.**

Love Revolves Around Others

"For all the animals of the field and forest are mine! The cattle on a thousand hills! And all the birds upon the mountains!"

Psalm 50:10-11

Richard Chamberlain's father, Chuck, lives here in Orange County. Years ago, he was riding through the hills of Laguna Canyon with John Crean, another great county resident. A large herd of cows was grazing on the hillside. "I'm worried about my cows," Chuck said, "I sure hope they get enough water to drink—it's been such a dry summer."

John looked surprised. "I didn't know you owned these cows and that ranch. I thought it was Irvine property." Chuck replied, "I own the cows, the hills, even this road. So do you. Every night as I look down on the twinkling lights of Laguna Beach, I say, 'I own it all; I'm just glad I don't have to manage it!' The Bible says 'the cattle and the fowls of the hills are mine,' God owns everything, and as His children, we do too. But we're just stewards. He trusts us with it."

That was the beginning of a change in John Crean's life. He learned to share his love and his material goods with others. He went on to give the first million dollar gift to the Crystal Cathedral and recently gave the church his beautiful ranch to be used as a retreat center.

Learn to share your love with others as God shares his love with you.

SOAR WITH THE
SURGE OF A NEW SPIRIT

Your Life Deserves To Be On A Higher Plane

"And those who have reason to be thankful should continually be singing praises to the Lord."
                                        James 5:13

Every morning before my children left for school, my family and I would repeat the lines of Ella Wheeler Wilcox,

I'm going to be happy today, though skies are cloudy or gray.

No matter what comes my way, I'm going to be happy today.

How you are going to feel today is under your control! As our children were growing up, we taught them a cybernetic reality, and that is, the brain is like a radio dial. All of the ideas that bombard you are like sound waves. You can switch the dial and pick up music, propaganda, or tension-producing messages. If our children were grumbling, cynical, crabby or depressed, we would say, "Come on, turn the dial."

Are you feeling down? *Then turn the dial.* Make the choice that is positive! Choose to feel good today.

**I will turn my dial to receive
God's positive sound waves.**

Your Life Deserves To Be On A Higher Plane

"When a man is gloomy, everything seems to go wrong; when he is cheerful, everything seems right."

Proverbs 15:15

If you think the turn-the-dial approach is too simplistic or unsophisticated, consider the findings in the book, *Feeling Good* by David D. Burns, M.D., University of Pennsylvania, Professor of Psychiatry. He states the most important thing in life is to feel good and have emotionally healthy feelings on a day-to-day, hour-to-hour basis. Good feelings will control everything else.

You can bury a stick, a tin can or a bone, but you can't bury a worm. And you can't bury your feelings. That is a psychological impossibility, because feelings will either peak out, leak out, squeak out, speak out, or shriek out! But, they will not be ignored. You have to deal with them.

It's a lot harder to harness the exit of an emotion than to control the entrance of an emotion. It's much more difficult to control your temper than to prevent yourself from anger in the first place. You can feel good on a daily basis when positive emotions are fed upon every day.

With a positive mental attitude, I can transform every situation that arises into a great possibility!

Your Life Deserves To Be On A Higher Plane

"The wages of sin is death, but the gift of God is eternal life."

Romans 6:23

The Ten Commandments are the fundamental principles which God gave to the human race to help us feel good. Ultimately, you know, feeling good is life, but many people—young, middle-aged, and old people—are dead because they don't feel good about themselves. This inability to feel good about yourself is unnecessary since God has provided a path to follow.

If you live by His principles, you will feel good. But if you, in your freedom or rebellion, resent them or ignore them, you will pay a price in your own emotional life.

The wages of negative thinking is the death of joy, hope, faith, and enthusiasm. We cause our own emotional death, not God. God brings the gift of eternal life! How does He give it to us? With ten positive principles.

The Ten Commandments are ten potent, emotional vitamins. Ten positive prescriptions. If you follow them, you will have health!

I eagerly follow the path that God who loves me set before me.

Your Life Deserves To Be On A Higher Plane

"For in six days the Lord made heaven, earth, and sea, and everything in them, and rested the seventh day; so he blessed the Sabbath day and set it aside for rest."

Exodus 20:11

Do you suffer from one of the terrible T's? Anyone of them can keep you from feeling good about yourself.

Tired. People who get tired usually get crabby. Maybe you're physically tired, and you need rest.

Tense. Are pressures mounting? If so, you need an experience of tranquility.

Tempted. We can feel very uneasy about ourselves when we are tempted.

Troubled. Are you suffering from grief, rejection or disappointment?

Torn. Sometimes we can get torn between the bad and the good. But it's even rougher when it's between the good and the better.

What does it take to live a triumphant, happy, successful, productive, creative, dynamic life? It takes the One-in-Seven Principle or the Fourth Commandment, *Remember to observe the Sabbath as a holy day.* Every seven days we need an in-depth encounter with our Maker. Then we will be renewed, refreshed, and ready to face the new week ahead.

To renew my spirit, I will rest in Jesus.

Your Life Deserves To Be On A Higher Plane

"The Lord says: Take warning and live, do no unnecessary work on the Sabbath day but make it a holy day. I gave this commandment to your fathers."

Jeremiah 17:21, 22

My wife and I discovered the One-in-Seven Principle twenty-six years ago. Since our marriage was the most important thing in our lives, we decided that every seven days we needed to be alone; and so established our Monday date night. No excuse is good enough for us to cancel our evening together.

God created the human being with an inspirational gas tank, and it only holds seven days. It needs to be refilled, refueled, and recharged. That's why God gave us the gift of the Sabbath. Once in every seven days you must attend a church where the tensions can be dissolved and you can have an effective spiritual renewal.

After church, spend some time listening to inspirational tapes, or reading the Bible. Have family discussions on how you can apply spiritual principles in your lives. Take time to be alone with God in silent prayer and worship. Lift up your heart and praise Him. Fill your home with songs of praise. The Lord has given his people another gift that produces life—the Sabbath!

Lord who made me and knows my every need, thank you for taking such good care of me.

Renew Your Soul—Before You Strive For Your Goal

"Keep the Sabbath day holy. This is my command."
> *Deuteronomy 5:12*

William Wolcott, the great English artist, came to New York in 1924 to record his impressions of that sky-scraper city. One morning in the architectural office of a colleague for whom he'd worked years before in England, he suddenly felt the urge to sketch. Seeing some paper on the desk, he asked if he could have it. The architectural colleague said, "That's not sketching paper, Mr. Wolcott. That's just ordinary wrapping paper." Wolcott, not wanting to lose the inspiration, reached out and said, "Nothing is ordinary if you know how to use it." And he took the drawing paper and made two sketches. One sold for $1,000; the other for $500. The principle: *Nothing is ordinary if you know how to use it.*

Sunday isn't just another day if you know how to use it. During this week, we will be looking more closely on how we can effectively utilize the Sabbath.

Every Sunday I begin anew!

Renew Your Soul—Before You Strive For Your Goal

"But the Sabbath was made to benefit man, and not man to benefit the Sabbath."

Mark 2:27

One day in seven. The Moslems set a day aside, Friday. The Jews set a day aside, Saturday. Most Christians set a day aside, Sunday, the first day of the week, to commemorate the Resurrection of Jesus Christ. The Sabbath is not an ordinary day if you know how to use it.

Traditionally, Sunday was a creative day of quietness for faith, fun and family, for the church and community, but something happened. During the past fifty years, we have seen a growing, deepening sense of depression in the wide-spread epidemic of emotional ailments like anxiety and stress, with its effect upon the human organism. This emotional epidemic of negative, mental, and spiritual problems in our country has risen sharply in proportion to our forsaking that one day in seven as a useful day for healing. We need to return to the restorative benefits of keeping the Sabbath.

As a nation, we need to relearn the joys of spending time with Jesus. Soak up His Sonlight. Let His rays of strength touch every part of you until you radiate energy. Fill your spirit deeply with his love.

On Sundays I will bask in Sonlight!

Renew Your Soul—Before You Strive For Your Goal

"Even during plowing and harvest times, work only six days, and rest on the seventh."
                                        Exodus 35:2

Sunday is a day of *rest*. I am profoundly indebted to Richard Neutra for the doctrine of bio-realism, which is that every human being is created with a built-in tranquilizing system. We have eyes to see the trees, hills and flowers; ears to hear birds singing, leaves rustling, and wind whispering; noses to smell the fragrances of flowers and new-mown grass; and skin to feel the caress of the sun and cool breezes. The biological reality is that God created this in order for these to be channels of tranquility entering your system.

We were not designed to live in a concrete jungle, and that is why we feel closer to God in the mountains, a park or a garden. Churches with their stained-glass windows, solid walls, and inspirational messages help to insulate you from the sights and sounds of our tension-producing world. They try to create a climate of sights and sounds where emotional tensions are released, and one can breathe in tranquility.

God has planned rest for me on Sunday.

Renew Your Soul—Before You Strive For Your Goal

"You must obey my Sabbath laws of rest, and reverence my Tabernacle, for I am the Lord."
Leviticus 26:2

Sunday is a day of *retreat.* A retreat from the pressures of the week.

When our oldest daughter, Sheila, was about four years old, her neighborhood playmate came to the house one Sunday asking if Sheila could come out and play. I wasn't prepared for that, and I said, "No, not today; but she can play tomorrow and every day the rest of the week, just not on Sunday."

That was the one day we could retreat as a family.

Sunday is a day to retreat and spend with myself, my family and my God.

Renew Your Soul—Before You Strive For Your Goal

"For this is a Sabbath of solemn rest, and in it you shall humble your souls and be filled with remorse; this time for atonement begins on the previous evening and goes on until the next evening."
Leviticus 23:32

Sunday is a day of *regrouping*. My greatest ideas have come to me while sitting in a church listening to a boring sermon. Since the sermon didn't get my attention, my mind wandered freely; and I began to think of what kind of life I had and where I was going. But God was leading the wandering. Even if you feel your pastor is boring, go anyway. It may be the best thing that ever happened to you! Let it be a day of regrouping.

Henry Ford hired an efficiency expert once to go through his plant. He said, "Find the non-productive people. Tell me who they are, and I will fire them." The expert reported, "Everytime I walk by this one employee's door, he is sitting with his feet propped up on the desk. When I go in, he stands, shakes hands, we exchange a few words; and when I leave, he props his feet upon his desk again. The man never does a thing." When Henry Ford learned the name of the man he said, "Well, I can't fire him. I pay him to do nothing but think."

You need one day in seven when you can have an experience in a church to do nothing but think.

I will take the opportunity of the Sabbath to let God lead my mind in wandering.

Renew Your Soul—Before You Strive For Your Goal

"This is the day the Lord has made. We will rejoice and be glad in it."

Psalms 118:24

Sunday is a day to *rejoice!* One day in seven you need an injection of positive emotion, to laugh, cry, feel love or a lift. Churches have the responsibility to provide a tremendous new surge of motivation and emotional energy. How can we deal with the negative traditions in our society and offer a sermon to fill your emotional needs? *By rejoicing!*

Early in the New Testament, the first Christians were inspired by the Holy Spirit to change their day of rest from Saturday to Sunday. The resurrection of Christ took place on Sunday, so it became a day for positive renewal!

I will rejoice in the Lord always!

Renew Your Soul—Before You Strive For Your Goal

"If you keep the Sabbath holy, not having your fun and business on that day, but enjoying the Sabbath and speaking of it with delight as the Lord's holy day, and honoring the Lord in what you do, not following your own desires and pleasure, nor talking idly, then the Lord will be your delight, and I will see to it that you ride high, and get your full share of the blessings I promised..."

Isaiah 58:13, 14

Life may be tough. Business may be rotten. Relationships may be sour. But you don't have to quit! People, pressures or problems may be keeping you from the success you want, but only you can say, "I quit."

Florence Chadwick wanted to be the first woman to swim from Catalina Island to Long Beach, a total of 26 miles. After many tortured, painful hours, unable to see the shoreline because of heavy fog, she quit. Afterwards, she learned she had only been a short distance from shore. She cried, "If only I had been able to see my goal, I could have made it."

We need Sundays. After six days of life's stresses, we need to rejoice, recharge and renew ourselves and our dreams. Sundays help us to see our goal and to keep us moving in the right direction.

Sunday, a very special gift from God.

Regroup and Restore—Before You Soar

"The man who knows right from wrong and has good judgment and common sense is happier than the man who is immensely rich!"

Proverbs 3:13

The Ten Commandments are not ten restrictions to keep you from enjoying life. Rather they are ten universal principles given to us by our Creator in order for us to more fully enjoy life.

At Hubert Humphrey's funeral, I said, "May we come like he did to the end of life with pride behind us, love around us, and hope ahead of us." I want you to live that way too, so pride will be behind you, not embarrassment or shame. The human being is less than the whole, healthy person he was meant to be unless and until he has a wonderful sense of self-dignity and self esteem.

We are children of God! And our Father has provided us with ten principles to help us live happier, fuller, more meaningful lives. How much He must love us to show us the way to live in peace and harmony with each other and with His world.

Peace and harmony in my life are in direct proportion to my obedience to God's principles.

Regroup and Restore—Before You Soar

"Honor your father and mother, that you may have a long, good life in the land the Lord your God will give you."

Exodus 20:12

The fifth Commandment is the only Commandment which promises long life. Since it holds the key to longevity, we would be wise to understand it.

In a poll George Gallup and I conducted, one of the questions asked was, "What is your attitude toward longevity?" It is shocking how many people don't want to live a long life. And equally shocking is when people say they don't want to grow old. People who are afraid to grow old don't have the sense of self-confidence, self-esteem and self-worth to believe that when they're old, they will still be exciting!

How many people do you think are alive today who are one hundred years or more? Amazingly, over 150,000!

Are you afraid of growing old? Are you afraid of the physical limitations that come with age? Just remember, whenever one door is closed, another is opened. There is an incredible number of options, alternatives and lifestyles open for possibility thinkers! A positive attitude can make growing old sensational!

The longer I live, the more Christ can do through me!

Regroup and Restore—Before You Soar

"You shall live a long, good life; like standing grain, you'll not be harvested until it's time!"
                                                                    Job 5:26

I met Robert Picking, president of the Picking Company, when he was in his mid-nineties. Founded by his grandfather, propagated by his father, and currently run by Bob Picking, the company is the last of the old copper shops in America still making their original products primarily by hand.

Bob was at work one day, as he is everyday, when he noticed some cast-off pieces of copper piled in the trash. They were not large enough for a skillet, pot or kettle. His workers told him these odd sizes were waste and would be melted down and thrown away. Bob responded, *"Nothing should be wasted. Nothing."*

To prove his point, he picked up one small piece and shaped it to form the scoop part of a shovel. Then he took a long narrow piece and rolled it to make a handle. He soldered the two pieces together into a beautiful work of art and autographed it. His life is proof that nothing should be wasted. Certainly not people! Creativity! Dreams!

Robert Picking never misses a day's work, and he never stops creating. Today he is over 100 years old!

Creativity is the real Fountain of Youth!

Regroup and Restore—Before You Soar

"I will be your God through all your lifetime, yes, even when your hair is white with age. I made you and I will care for you. I will carry you along and be your Savior."

Isaiah 46:4

When you realize you probably will live a long life, your perspective on many things changes. Your perspective on goals will broaden. Education will never become a closed door because of age. So you're 65; start a new career! When you look back on it, you'll be glad you did.

A member of this church bought 20 acres of land on a time-payment plan for development. She said, "I want to build tennis courts, spas, and a beautiful conference center to be used as a retreat. So, Dr. Schuller, if you and your ministers want to be my guests, you'll be welcome." Do you know how old this possibility thinker is? Over 80!

When people ask her why she would want to begin a long-term project at her age, her answer is that a question like that indicates a problem with attitude.

It's true! Get set to live a long life!

With Christ, you can begin again at any age!

Regroup and Restore—Before You Soar

"If you are filled with light within, with no dark corners, then your face will be radiant too, as though a floodlight is beamed upon you."
                                        Luke 11:35

What is youth or age? It's measured more by the mind than by the skin. I've seen some college students in their twenties walk like tired old people. Some act like there isn't a spark of energy left in them. On the other hand, I know people in their 70's and 80's who walk quickly, think fast and are filled with energy! The difference is in their heads. It's possibility thinking!

People who are young at heart are possibility thinkers. When they see possibilities, they get involved. They set goals and make decisions. They start projects. They have a purpose for living. They can't wait to get up in the morning!

The key to longevity is in the fifth commandment, "Honor your father and your mother..." You honor your father when you follow in his steps, not necessarily following his occupation, but at a deeper level, holding the same faith in our Lord. That's how the commandment has to be interpreted, because it was given to believers, the Godly children of Godly parents.

**Jesus does not see the wrinkles:
He looks for the twinkles!**

Regroup and Restore—Before You Soar

"I will satisfy him with a full life and give him my salvation."

Psalms 91:16

If you want to live a long life, enjoy dynamic religious vitality! Science has proven that people who live by positive religion, live longer. When the brain is stimulated by positive emotions, it releases endorphins. These are chemicals generated by possibility thinking. Scientists at the UCLA Department of Psychiatry have isolated dozens of these brain chemicals.

At the University of Pennsylvania, Division of Psychiatry, Dr. Burns has taken depressed patients of equal magnitude and put some under Freudian therapy, some under pharmaceutical therapy (giving drugs to lift the depression), and others into mood therapy. Mood therapy is the process where the staff does nothing more than program the patients minds with positive thinking. The result of the test? The health rate of mood therapy far outweighed Freudian analysis or chemical therapy. This study is documented in the book, *Feeling Good,* by Dr. Burns.

Now we have scientific data to support it. Possibility thinking works!

Jesus, I give you permission to reprogram my mind with your positive thoughts.

Regroup and Restore—Before You Soar

"The godly shall be firmly planted in the land, and live there forever."

Psalm 37:29

We are having economical problems today because people in our government assumed that everyone would die around 65 years of age, and that's not happening! It's going to get worse in the next 25 to 50 years, and I've reached the point where I've decided not to count on Social Security.

A statistic I read stated that all those on Social Security will, in the year 2030, have accumulated a net worth, based on current interest rates, of about $437,000. Almost half a million dollars!

Another statistic: If the money spent on smoking cigarettes was put into an IRA account, in 2030 it would be worth $1,130,000. More than double!

President Ronald Reagan made an interesting comment. He referred to Abraham, who lived to be nearly 150 years old. His wife was only a few years younger. The president said, "Can you imagine how rich he would have been if he'd opened an IRA account?"

We can develop a plan of savings and investment geared toward becoming financially independent. Take a new look at how long you're going to live and plan for it!

My security now and for eternity is in the Lord!

Fly Farther on Wings of Faith

"God declares us 'not guilty' of offending him if we trust in Jesus Christ, who in his kindness freely takes away our sins."

Romans 3:24

I promise you if you truly make a decision to live by faith in Jesus Christ, it will make you healthier! How does Jesus Christ fit into the concept of longevity? Because He calls us to the adventure of possibility thinking. First, He releases us from our sin and guilt. Second, He offers us forgiveness, and then we can feel good about ourselves. Released from shame through Christ's forgiveness, we are free to discover self-esteem.

When that process takes place, a person finds personal internal security, and then dares to love!

Some people die in fire. Some people die in flame.

But most people perish inch by inch playing at little games.

How do you live long? By having a dynamic faith! And you receive a dynamic faith when you make the decision to believe in Jesus Christ!

Because of Jesus, I am free to live, laugh and love!

Fly Farther on Wings of Faith

"You shall give honor and respect to the elderly, in the fear of God. I am Jehovah."

Leviticus 19:32

How does a positive religion, or the faith of our forefathers, contribute to longevity? By producing a different kind of society. Anthropology teaches there are two basic kinds of societies. One is where the young attack the old. The young buck will attack the old buck and wound him until he falls. When the wolves come in for the kill, the young buck takes over the herd. In this society of living creatures, the young attack the old. Some human beings live by that animal instinct. They attack the old people, discard them, and then take over control.

The other kind of society is where the young respect the old. In fact, they revere them. They try to preserve the life of the old people because they see an accumulation of wisdom from which they can learn. Obviously, this kind of society is going to live collectively longer and is the one keeping the Lord's Commandment!

The lines on the faces of the elderly indicate the treasures of wisdom stored within.

Fly Farther on Wings of Faith

"He gives food to every living thing, for his loving kindness continues forever."

Psalm 136:25

A dynamic religion produces a different lifestyle. The truth is that if we live by the Ten Commandments, odds are we won't be shot while robbing a bank, or by a jealous spouse. Ages of rock stars involved in the drug culture are very low. Many of them die in their late twenties and early thirties from drug overdoses.

The Jewish people had very strict dietary laws, which may have contributed to their long life spans more than we know. At the University of California Irvine, Medical School, very interesting research is being conducted using rats. The older the rat becomes, the more it produces fats from a normal diet, and the increase of the fats seems to be in direct proportion to the rapidity of the aging process.

Modern science is proving that many of the old Levitical laws actually added longevity to the lives of practicing Jews. Even though we don't follow all of these old laws, Christians still uphold the importance of taking care of our bodies, which are the temples of our souls. Because your body is a part of you, and you are created in the image of God, you are a worthy creature! A valued creature! You must not do anything to the body that would be dangerous; and, of course, this attitude will produce a longer life!

**Food restores my body
like prayer restores my soul!**

Fly Farther on Wings of Faith

"But they that wait upon the Lord shall renew their strength. They shall mount up with wings like eagles; they shall run and not be weary; they shall walk and not faint."

Isaiah 40:31

Sigmund Freud said it, and he was right—there is within every one of us countering wills; the will to die, and the will to live. Under stress, extreme anxiety, or in a setting of enormous frustration, a depression can conquer you to the point where the will to die is stronger than the will to live.

But when the depressed person discovers a positive faith in a caring, loving God, then the will to live surfaces; and with it, the faith and hope to continue! Like an unexpected gust of wind under the weary wings of a tired sparrow, in a wearisome moment on a long and painful flight, the little creature is lifted and suddenly flies and soars with the surge of a new spirit. And the will to live is strong! Dynamic positive-thinking, self-esteem centered religion prolongs life!

My will to live is strong because I know that with God all things are possible!

Fly Farther on Wings of Faith

"So now, since we have been made right in God's sight by faith in his promises, we can have real peace with him because of what Jesus Christ our Lord has done for us."

Romans 5:1

Rene DuBos, a great scientist, once said, "The human being has an infinite capacity to adjust downward," to which I replied, "Adjustment is always a downward movement. The upward movement is never an adjustment, it is always a commitment!" That commitment comes through self-esteem, pride and human worth.

In the last article written before his death, Rene DuBos said what I'm trying to say. If you lose your pride in being human, you lose your self-esteem. When that happens you'll no longer believe that it's possible to solve the problems. Self-esteem produces possibility thinking. Remove self-dignity and you remove self-confidence. But adopt the faith of your father's and get set for a long life!

I am the King's kid! I am important because I walk with Jesus!

Fly Farther on Wings of Faith

"The Lord is good. When trouble comes, He is the place to go! And He knows everyone who trusts in Him!"

Nahum 1:17

One summer I was privileged to go on a tour to Israel with eighty Hour of Power viewers. I loved it, because I love people, and I was able to get to know each of my fellow travelers. I found out that everybody had a dream, and everybody had a hurt.

There were these two beautiful girls; their brother had been murdered some years back, and it had been a crushing tragedy. But they knew they'd find an even more beautiful faith than they already had when they went to the Holy Land. And they did!

There was a lovely woman on the trip. Years before, her husband had died, leaving her with small children to raise alone. She too had put her faith in God, and He had carried her through.

Have faith in God—He'll carry you through.

Fly Farther on Wings of Faith

"...so if your faith remains strong after being tried in the test tube of fiery trials, it will bring you much praise and glory and honor on the day of His return."

I Peter 1:7

I met a family recently who told me of a severe testing of their faith. They had three beautiful daughters, and were looking forward to the birth of a new baby. They were hoping for a boy, and God gave them a son.

It didn't take long, though, before they realized that their little boy was different—brain damaged. It was a terrible time for them. They were angry, bitter, full of self pity. But they kept their faith. They kept praying.

And God answered them. "I will teach you a new dimension of love!", He said. God used their faith to enrich their lives with a new and deeper love than they had known before. He used them as a powerful witness to others.

My life can become a testimony of my mountain-moving faith in Jesus!

Soar Like An Eagle

"All the animals of field and forest are mine! The cattle on a thousand hills! And all the birds upon the mountains!"

Psalms 50:10, 11

The Commandment that teaches us the value of life is "Thou Shall Not Kill." God looks upon all of life on this planet as something with infinite potential. We say, "Any fool can count the seeds in an apple, but only God can count all of the apples in one seed." God values the potential in each seed and in each life.

Asa Skinner was a member of my first church in Chicago, Illinois. He was an active executive who underwent brain surgery, and I wondered how he'd be able to tolerate the long recovery period. I called on him shortly after he was dismissed from the hospital. His wife met me and told me his spirits were high. "Come on," she said, "you can see why."

I found him in his tiny backyard, sitting in a chair wearing his bathrobe, and his head was all bandaged in white. His wife told me he was studying. As I approached him I noticed he was looking at the ground through binoculars. He was watching the ants build a home and transport material. He pointed at a nest the wasps built, and one that a robin was building. The ants, the wasps, the robin. He said, "Dr. Schuller, this world is throbbing with life, and all of life is so beautiful; it's a pity that a single insect has to die."

Develop in me, Lord, an appreciation for all your creatures.

Soar Like An Eagle

"Then God said, 'Let us make a man—someone like ourselves, to be the master of all life upon the earth and in the skies and in the seas."

Genesis 1:26

Albert Schweitzer had a tremendous doctrine of reverence for life. He thought it was the universal principle from which everything else evolved. There were those, however, who felt that he took it too far. In fact, as a result of his protection for rodents and bacteria-carrying insects, there were some problems with infection.

We do not take the position of those Hindus in India who allow human beings to die of starvation while they allow the rats to survive on the grain that has been shipped there by Americans. In their religion no animals, not even a rat, may be killed, even though it consumes the limited food resulting in the death of human beings.

In Christianity, and in Judaism, we have great reverence for all life, but the highest form of all life that we revere is human life. And that's why in Judaic-Christian culture, we say it's not a question of whether or not it's right to kill. The real question is: What life form should be given the privilege and priority to live?

Thank you, Father that we are made in your image.

Soar Like An Eagle

"And now you are free from your old master, sin; and you have become slaves to your new master, righteousness."

Romans 6:18

When a person loses self-esteem, he loses his life; either by suicide or through a degenerate lifestyle. We all know that the alcoholic is really trying to destroy himself because he can't cope. The people who seek relief with chemical addictions are choosing a lifestyle that's self-destructive. They kill themselves by killing their awareness of the world around them.

"Thou Shall Not Kill," means don't undervalue yourself. Give yourself credit for being intelligent, creative, and inventive. You have the freedom to make decisions. You have the ability to solve problems. You have the capacity to sort things out, and the potential to handle any challenges you may face in relationships, marriage, business, finances, or even in your own health.

Value yourself and your life very highly. When you value yourself, you will in turn value others. We project our own feelings on other persons, so we must choose positive responses instead of negative ones!

Because God loves me, I can love me!

Soar Like An Eagle

*"Under the laws of Moses the rule was, 'If you
kill, you must die.' But I have added to that rule,
and tell you that if you are only angry, even in
your own home, you are in danger of judgment!
If you call your friend an idiot, you are in danger
of being brought before the court. And if you curse
him, you are in danger of the fires of hell."*
                                    Matthew 5:21, 22

Jesus made the above statement. It means you
destroy a human life when you insult someone,
demean him, strip him of his dignity, embarrass
him, shame him, and leave him humiliated. The
positive fulfillment of this Commandment is to tell
people how great they can be if they will only let
Jesus Christ and His love live in their lives. That
is Christ's answer. It is His way of saying that the
fulfillment of this Commandment is the development of self-esteem in people.

Every problem has a positive and negative
solution. We have to learn to choose the positive
solutions! To look on the positive side of people's
actions. To see the love of Christ in everyone!

**Today, I give love and encourage self-love
in the people I meet.**

Soar Like An Eagle

"If you love your neighbor as much as you love yourself you will not want to harm or cheat him, or kill him or steal from him. And you won't sin with his wife or want what is his, or do anything else the Ten Commandments say is wrong. All ten are wrapped up in this one, to love your neighbor as you love yourself."

Romans 13:9

Jesus Christ teaches us to value life in ourselves as well as in others.

Would a farm be perfect just because it didn't have any weeds? By no means. It's not enough for a farm to be void of weeds. The land must be productive!

And so it is with people. If you go through life and never kill, never hurt, never injure, are you a perfect person? It's not enough not to kill. We must be productive with the kind of love that reaches out to people everywhere. Instead of insulting them, we put our arms around them and say, "God loves you and so do I."

If you look upon every person as having tremendous potential, you'll love life. You'll love God, yourself and your neighbor. With that much love, what a beautiful community of human beings we can become.

My love for others must bear fruit! I will actively love my brothers and sisters in Christ!

COME ALIVE—NOW!

Be Aware of Life

"He will swallow up death in victory."
                                        Isaiah 25:8

Is Jesus Christ alive today? The answer is a resounding *yes!* Those who witnessed and experienced His crucifixion and then saw Him three days later, walking, talking, *alive,* made strong note of it. They recorded it in the Holy Bible. For 2,000 years that record has remained intact; and for that reason there is no philosophical, psychological, idealogical or theological truth that I believe more convincingly than the reality of the resurrection of Jesus Christ.

Christ is alive! Another important question is: Are *you* alive! *Really alive?* The truth is, many of us are not. Someone really alive has a heightened, sharpened sensitivity and a perception of reality around him. Awareness is the beginning of being really alive.

How do we become aware? Through the *living* Jesus Christ, who is totally involved with us in the celebration of life!

Because Jesus lives in me, I can come alive!

Be Aware of Life

"For with thee is the fountain of life: in thy light shall we see light."

Psalm 36:9

Tragically enough, too many people are not aware of the world around them. They don't see the trees, hear the birds, or absorb the fragrances. Life goes on about them, but they aren't even conscious of it because subliminal negative emotions and anxieties paralyze them. They are physically alive, but emotionally dead.

If you are in that state of mind or heart, the *living* Christ can heal you of the negative emotions which keep you from being aware, loving, involved, vital and enthusiastic.

Jesus Christ is alive! He is aware of you and me. He loves us. He is willing to get involved in our lives. The cross is proof! And He is the source of our strength and energy.

Take a walk with Jesus today. Create a mental picture of taking His hand in yours and walking in your neighborhood, at a park, the beach, or anywhere. Then look with Him at the trees, flowers, sky, and everything else in His world. Look more closely at petals, insects, rocks or shells. Jesus can bring a new awareness of life into you today.

Even in familiar surroundings, I can see things I never saw before as Jesus leads me into a new life.

Fall in Love with Life

"You search the Scriptures, for you believe they give you eternal life. And the Scriptures point to me!"

John 5:39

During my first visit to the People's Republic of China, I noticed the little red books, *The Great Sayings of Mao Tse-tung,* were being distributed freely. On my last visit there, however, they were not being passed out anymore.

Yet 2,000 years later, millions of people all over the world still look to the great sayings of Jesus Christ for direction. What's even more important, they look to Him for *action! Involvement! Life!*

To love life is to love Jesus Christ!

Fall in Love with Life

"But the water I give them becomes a perpetual spring within them, watering them forever with eternal life."

John 4:14

Long before he was a Christian, B. J. Thomas became famous with the record, "Raindrops Keep Falling on My Head." From that success, B. J. got involved with narcotics so deeply that he almost died from an overdose. His marriage started falling apart. His entire life started coming unglued. Then, he met Jesus Christ and was literally turned into a new person!

No matter where you are coming from, no matter where you are emotionally right now, God can reach you. He will touch you because He really cares. *He loves you.*

Do you know Jesus? Are you one of His followers? Have you accepted Him into your life and into your heart as your Friend and Savior? Just being in church does not make you a Christian. You become a Christian when you admit, "Christ, I need you. I want you. I love you."

Fall in love with Jesus, the lifegiver.

Fall in Love with Life

"No I will not abandon you or leave you as orphans in the storm—I will come to you."
                                        John 14:18

As a Scottish lassie lay dying, someone asked her, "Lassie, where are you going?"

She replied, "I'm going to heaven."

"How can you be so sure that's where you're going?"

"Because He promised. He said, 'I will not leave you.' That's good enough for me."

The other person queried, "But what if He forgets His promise?"

The lassie said, "He'd lose more than I. I'd only lose my soul, but He'd lose His honor."

Jesus is a man of honor and He has promised not to leave us comfortless. That's good enough for me, too!

Christians deal with sorrow, struggle, and suffering. A famous poet said, "In love's service, only broken hearts will do." Only the person who has been hurt can really care. When you have been deeply hurt and have experienced real suffering, you can then begin to care about others who are hurting.

**Today I will let Jesus love someone
through my heart.**

Fall in Love with Life

"I give them eternal life and they shall never perish. No one shall snatch them from me."
                                        John 10:28

Critics accuse possibility-thinking Christians of proclaiming a "Pollyanna" faith. That's untrue. Christians are not spared from pain, stress, or problems.

Kathy Gill, the Manager of Material Control for our entire ministry, discovered that she has leukemia. After calling on her in the hospital, I went to the warehouse to speak with all the employees. A great crowd of us, Mexicans, Orientals, Blacks and Whites, held hands and prayed for Kathy.

The next time I saw her she asked me to make a poster for her with the statement: There is No Gain Without Some Pain!

Here is a beautiful sentence I've remembered, "When everything looks hopeless, suddenly a ray of light comes from somewhere." In times of stress, struggle and suffering, when you think you can handle no more, Jesus comes, like the sun breaking through the clouds.

Jesus does the mending, which frees me to do the tending.

Fall in Love with Life

"Keep up the good work and don't get discouraged, for you will be rewarded."
                                        II Chronicles 15:7

Penny Cotton, a young woman who attended the National Women's Conference at the Crystal Cathedral, suffered a stroke when she was twenty-seven years old. It almost killed her and left her paralyzed. Because of this paralysis, she did not want to live, and began to plan her suicide.

On Sunday morning, she tuned in *Hour of Power*; and through the happy faces and joyful music, she received hope. That started some new thoughts, and shortly thereafter, she became a possibility thinker. Why? Because she committed her life to Jesus Christ and dared to believe she could earn her own way in life and not be dependent on others.

That's exactly what she did! She became a life insurance saleswoman. Still severely handicapped, but in deep gratitude to God, she saved $500 to purchase a star which hangs from the ceiling of the Cathedral. Sometime later, she said to me, "I'm just a little pebble. Some people have given a million dollars to this church, and it took me such a long time to save up $500." I replied, "If there were no pebbles, there would be no beaches. The pebbles make up the beaches of the world!"

**God and I are a majority and
all things become possible.**

Fall in Love with Life

"The thief's purpose is to steal, kill and destroy. My purpose is to give life in all its fullness."
John 10:10

Here's a story of a woman who moved to the desert with her husband and her life became very unhappy. She wrote to her mother, "I'm going to leave my husband. I can't stand living in the California desert. It's awful, there is only desert sagebrush and Indians. They don't seem interested in me and I can't relate to them either." Her mother wrote back, "Two people sit behind prison bars. One sees mud, and the other sees stars. Honey, look for the stars."

So the woman tried by getting interested in the Indians. She found there was so much to learn! Then she got interested in the desert flowers and rocks, and it became the most enriching time of her life.

When life seems boring, sometimes it is only our view of it that needs to be corrected. Jesus can help us to have a positive perspective on life!

**If we want to find Jesus,
we have to look up!**

Fall in Love with Life

"Tell those who are rich not to be proud and not to trust in their money, which will soon be gone, but their pride and trust should be in the living God who always richly gives us all we need for our enjoyment."

I Timothy 6:17

Christ changes us by changing our perspective of our situation. Charlie Edison told this story about his dad.

Thomas Edison was sixty-seven years old when he was financially wiped out. All of the Edison industries amounted to two million dollars when a major fire struck. Charlie recalls watching his dad shivering in the winter wind while he looked at the fire consuming his property. All he had was two hundred thousand dollars insurance and two million dollars were going up in flames.

Thomas Edison said, "Charlie, call your mother! She's never going to see a sight like this as long as she lives!" Charlie recalled, "I saw my dad standing there looking at the ashes—sixty-seven years of his life all gone up in smoke. He looked at me and said, "Charlie, there is one wonderful thing about disasters. They burn up all your mistakes. You're free to start again!" Three months later Thomas Edison delivered the phonograph, and the rest is history.

It's not important to know what the future holds. But it's vital that we know who holds the future!

Become Involved in Other Lives

"Love holds no resentment."
I Corinthians 13:5

How do you handle the people whose lives, behavior, or attitudes you do not approve of? How do you handle the non-approvable persons, experiences or situations? To sum it up, there are several alternatives.

Reticence. You simply avoid the issue or the person if possible.

Resistance. You begin to stiffen up inside and bristle within. You try to keep yourself protected from an involvement with that person.

Retreat. You make an excuse and split. You quit going to church, or separate from your spouse.

Rebellion. It might be verbal or take some other form. We all have our own contrived, subconscious or conscious ways of rebelling.

Resentment. Non-approval at its most negative, intense level takes this form.

Resentment can be handled in a positive way. We just need a broader definition of loving others.

Today I will glorify God by how I handle my relationships with others.

Become Involved in Other Lives

"When you are praying, first forgive anyone you are holding a grudge against, so that your Father in heaven will forgive you your sins too."
                              Mark 11:25

How do you handle the experiences that you just can't approve? Try repentance. Resentment is the emotional signal that requires repentance. You may feel your resentment is justified, but did you know it is a biological reality that resentment is destructive to your health? There is no human being alive on planet earth who can harbor resentment without injuring himself and those around him. And if you're knowingly injuring yourself to any degree, it has to be a sin.

You may have excellent reasons for your resentment. Then, so much more the reason why you must meet it with repentance! Meet the non-approving resentment-generating experience or person with repentance.

Perhaps you need to forgive someone. Seek the Lord's help. Once you are willing to forgive, your heart will be flooded with His forgiveness of you!

**Thank you, Lord, for helping me now
to forgive others as you have forgiven me.**

Become Involved in Other Lives

"Dear friends, never avenge yourselves. Leave that to God, for he has said that he will repay those who deserve it."

Romans 12:19

Resentment produces three sins. The first one is not trusting God Almighty with His job of executing justice.

If you have resentment, probably it's because you feel you've been treated unfairly. Maybe you have been down-right victimized. An overpowering sense of justice gives birth to this sense of resentment. In this case, resentment becomes your way to mete out justice. But that's a sin!

The Bible teaches us that vengeance belongs to God. At no point in it does God ever command us to execute that kind of justice against sins. We must trust Him. He is already executing justice. You can be sure the person who has victimized you is already paying the price within his own conscience, heart or mind. Maybe you don't see any evidence of it, but *he* will! God has His own ways of executing justice. He can! He is! He will! And He'll do a much better job than you or I.

I trust you, Lord!

Become Involved in Other Lives

"No, dear brothers, I am still not all I should be but I am bringing all my energies to bear on this one thing: Forgetting the past and looking forward to what lies ahead..."

Philippians 3:13

A teacher took his art class to a hill where the sunsets were unusually beautiful. As the colors broke (purples, reds, pinks, oranges, yellows, golds and greens) the teacher walked among the students, and he noticed one student busily painting a shingle on a barn in the valley. He was tediously painting the shingles on the roof. The teacher turned his attention to the gorgeous sunset and said, "if you don't forget the shingles, the sunset will be gone; and you will have missed it."

The point is, don't get so locked into the shingles you miss the sunset. Don't concentrate on negatives which are resentments and miss the positives which are the benefits of repentance.

People are beautiful yet different, like every sunset. I will focus on the positive and see beauty!

Become Involved in Other Lives

"So warmly welcome each other into the church, just as Christ has warmly welcomed you; then God will be glorified."

Romans 15:7

The third sin of repentance is failing to see the positive side of a negative. Every negative situation has some positive element in it. No one is totally bad. If we don't see the good in people, we need to repent—for not having enough love inside. It isn't easy, but I can assure you that Jesus Christ never fails to give you the love you need if you ask Him. With His love in you, it becomes easier to not only see the good in others, but to really love them.

Lord, give me the grace to love a saint as much as you love a sinner.

Become Involved in Other Lives

"In everything you do, stay away from complaining and arguing, so that no one can speak a word of blame against you."

Philippians 2:14

In a monastery on Mount Serat in Spain, one of the requirements of the religious order is that the monks must maintain perpetual silence. Only after two years are they allowed to speak, and then only two words. Two more years of silence, and they're allowed two more words, and so it goes every two years.

A young initiate, who had spent his first two years at the monastery, was called by his superior to make his first two-word statement. "Bed hard," he said. Two years later his two words were, "Food bad." After the next two years, he said, "I quit." The superior looked at him and said, "It doesn't surprise me. All you've done since you've been here is complain, complain, complain."

How do you react when someone complains? Do you see a person's heart or the unpleasantness he may be expressing? How would Jesus respond?

Today I will be careful not to complain.

Become Involved in Other Lives

"Do for others what you want them to do for you."
Matthew 7:12

Resentment is the most dangerous reaction to a non-approving experience, situation or person. In one of my books I wrote, "Are you carrying resentments? Fears? Anxieties? How much do you suffer because you will not forgive someone who hurt you deeply? How many sunny days are turning gray by your angry mind, seething, quarreling in fantasy-bouts with your adversary, an ex-spouse, a relative, neighbor, customer, client or clerk? Do you have ulcers, arthritis, high blood pressure, or heart problems because you will not forgive? And how many people are developing wrinkles in their skin that will become permanent creases, monuments to the fact they spent most of their lives thinking angry thoughts until the frowns work their way irreducibly and permanently into their faces? How many friends did you once have who no longer talk to you because you developed a reputation of pouting, grumbling, and complaining?

If you answer yes to any of these questions, it's time to let go!

I am letting go of all my resentments toward others, and will treat them the way I would like to be treated.

Vitality—You Can Have It

"So exercise yourself spiritually and practice being a better Christian, because that will help you not only now in this life, but in the next life too."
                                        I Timothy 4:8

A man once dreamed he died and immediately entered a large room with a huge banquet table filled with a great variety of food. People seated at the table were obviously hungry, but their chairs were five feet from the table and they were somehow riveted to their seats. Furthermore, their arms were too short to reach the food on the table.

Everyone was fighting, quarreling and pushing each other trying to get the only five-foot-long spoon. Finally, in an awful scene, a strong bully took the spoon, picked up some food, and turned it to feed himself, only to discover the spoon was so long that as he held it out, he could not touch his mouth. The food fell off. Immediately, someone else grabbed the spoon, tried to feed himself and again failed. The man observing his own dream said to his guide, "It is hell to have food and not be able to eat it." The guide replied, "This *is* hell, but you do not belong here. Come with me."

And they went to another room, exactly like the first in all respects. Yet these people had a satisfied expression on their faces. Here, no one was fighting for the spoon. In fact, one man held the five-foot handle and fed another person. They took turns feeding each other, and all were satisfied. The guide said, "Welcome to Heaven."

I cannot help someone else without greatly helping myself.

Vitality—You Can Have It

"Share each other's troubles and problems, and so obey our Lord's command."
                                        Galatians 6:2

Every state has laws. Every country has legal statutes. Every city has ordinances. Since we belong to the Kingdom of Jesus Christ, we are obligated to live by the law of Christ, which is that selfishness turns life into a burden, and unselfishness turns a burden into life.

If you want to be fed, you have to feed someone else. If you want happiness, look for someone who needs the lift that only you can give. If you really *care,* you will *carry* somebody else's burdens and in the process you'll discover the ultimate secret of happiness.

Everybody wants to be happy. I've observed in the world today, many people are trying to reach happiness with selfishness, but they end up in a hell on earth. Others who try to obtain joy by following this law of Christ, by helping somebody else, find their connection to joy is eternal!

The way to happiness is to remember "caring is carrying."

Vitality—You Can Have It

*"Don't think only of yourself. Try to think of the
other fellow, too, and what is best for him."*
                                    I Corinthians 10:24

Think of two words: cobwebs and cables.

In your mind's eye picture cobwebs, in a tree,
on a plant, or in a dark corner of a room. Now
imagine the steel cables that hold buildings
together while they're being erected. What a
difference there is between cobwebs and cables.

If you choose the selfish approach to life, your
happiness will be connected by cobwebs. The
slightest little upsetting experience will shatter your
joy and bring you to tears. But if you live by the
law of Christ and help people who have burdens,
you'll be connected to joy by cables!

Selfishness turns a life into a burden. Unselfishness turns burdens into life. So, the secret, of
course, is to care. And caring becomes carrying.

**I will reach out my hand
and help someone else today.**

Vitality—You Can Have It

"Yes indeed, it is good when you truly obey our Lord's command, 'You must love and help your neighbors just as much as you love and take care of yourself.'"

James 2:8

We had a custom in our little, Dutch, Iowa community. If somebody became ill, my mother would bake a pie, cookies, or a loaf of bread and take it to that neighbor. So, I was accustomed to sharing food.

But I had never before heard of what they do in the Bahamas. In the villages at suppertime, everybody cooks their own meals at the same time; and as you walk down the street, you smell the delicious fragrances in the air. But before they sit down in each home to eat, the doors open and the people walk out with plates. They have made an abundance, so they take a plate of food to share with a neighbor. And the neighbor shares with them. It's like a potluck every night!

It reminds me of when my wife and I go out to dinner and I order a different entree than she does. If mine is very good, I want her to have some, so I offer her a taste. If she responds affirmatively, I cut a piece and share it with her. And she gives me a portion of hers.

When we really care, we're willing to share.

Vitality—You Can Have It

"Dear friends, let us practice loving each other, for love comes from God and those who are loving and kind show that they are children of God, and that they are getting to know him better."
I John 4:7

My daughter, Carol, has only one leg as a result of an accident a few years ago. One night she was returning home and spotted our family dog, Poco, beside the road near our house. She was shocked to see him lying in the street apparently dead. She heard a whimper and on one foot hopped over to him. She tried to lift the weight of the injured dog but lost her balance and fell. She got back up, but with only one foot, she couldn't carry the weight of the animal.

Just then a car came by and the driver said, "May I help?" Weeping, Carol replied, "My dog's been hurt, and I know what it's like to get hurt when you've been hit by a car at night. Please help me." The driver picked up little Poco and put him on the front seat of Carol's car. With proper care and attention to his broken jaw, Poco recovered.

This story is a good example of *when you care, you carry.*

Lord, open my eyes to the hurts and needs of others so that I may help.

Vitality—You Can Have It

"It is God at work in you giving you the will and the power to achieve His purpose."
Philippians 2:13

How can you carry someone in such a way that you display a care which makes him stronger and more liberated instead of more enslaved to you and your helping hand? How does God carry you? He does it by motivating us instead of manipulating us! He motivates by giving us a dream, then a desire. Someone said to me recently, "I want to do this so much, but as a Christian I don't think I should." I asked why. He said, "Because I think it's my will, not the Lord's." And I responded, "Look, if you were God and you had to motivate people, you'd probably give them the desire to do it. Just because you want to do it doesn't mean it's not God's will. You're a Christian. Because you want to do it, it's probably an indication it *is* God's will."

I suppose one of the hardest jobs in the world is to carry someone's burdens without turning him into a weaker person. Welfare is needed in our society, but how do we give welfare and strengthen instead of weaken people? I believe we can carry each other's burdens while we strengthen ourselves by sharing the belief that God has a plan for each of us, and we have the potential to fulfill it. All we need to do is trust in Him, in the ideas He gives us, and in the direction He leads us. Then we will not only become strong, but we will never lose hope.

Seeing my part in your plan, Father, produces such freedom, excitement, and vitality because You are in control and You do not fail.

Vitality—You Can Have It

"And I am sure that God who began the good work within you will keep right on helping you grow in his grace until his task within you is finally finished on that day when Jesus Christ returns."
Philippians 1:6

God gives you a dream and the desire, then He carries you to strength and success by seeing you through to completion, to the top of the mountain!

Once I was in San Francisco on a cable car, and half-way up the hill it lost power. Everybody had to get out and walk the rest of the way. Many fear this in their own lives. They are afraid, because they fear the power will run out before they get to the top of the hill.

Strength to see you through to the end is what God promises and provides. God carries us with a *dream,* a *decision,* a *desire,* and finally the *determination* to trust Him.

The assurance that God will see me through releases vitality.

Enthusiasm for Life—Here's How

"Be delighted with the Lord. Then he will give you all your heart's desires."

Psalm 37:4

The Christian religion does not always come across as a positive faith. Regretably, sometimes it has been interpreted and perceived as a negative religion. I believe this is the result of a misinterpretation of some of the sayings of Jesus.

Jesus Christ was the most positive person who ever lived! Nothing is greater than meeting positive people. This summer I was in China where I met a vivacious 83-year-old lady from Arkansas. She was a charming, delightful, positive person. I commented once on how enthusiastic she was. She replied, "Ever since I began watching Hour of Power, I've become so positive. Even at my age I have four boyfriends." Her eyes twinkled as she continued, "I begin my day with Will Power, then I take a walk with Arthur Ritis. I come back with Charlie Horse and spend my evening with Ben Gay." Now that's what I call positive thinking!

Jesus was a positive person; and Christianity, rightly understood, is a positive faith!

Jesus is a positive leader of a positive faith.

Enthusiasm for Life—Here's How

"If any man would be my disciple, let him deny himself, take up his cross and follow me."
Matthew 16:24

The road to the cross is the way to enthusiasm. Does that sound like a contradiction? Actually that concept has been grossly misinterpreted and distorted by negative-thinking theologians and interpreters. When I reviewed the science of hermeneutics, which is discovering principles from interpretations of statements, the most important principle is to observe who is speaking and where he is coming from.

In Matthew 16:24, I believe Jesus is pointing to three principles of dynamic living:

Get involved!
Make a commitment!
Follow through!

All three are success-producing, enthusiasm-generating principles. Jesus is saying to be a Christian, you have to be a good advertisement. Be enthusiastic!

Jesus is an example of dynamic living.

Enthusiasm for Life—Here's How

*"'If any of you wants to be my follower,' he told
them, 'you must put aside your own pleasures and
shoulder your cross, and follow me closely.'"*
Mark 8:34

What does Christ mean when he says "deny
yourself" (Matthew 16:24) and "put aside your own
pleasures" (Mark 8:34)? Self-denial means involvement. The "I am" will always determine the "I can."
If you say, "I'm not attractive," or "I'm not intelligent,"
or "I'm not successful," you are denying a profound
theological truth. *Self-affirmation is the pathway to
self-denial.*

When you believe in yourself, you begin to
volunteer. When you put yourself down, you withdraw.
The non-self-loving person is too empty of self-worth
to give any away. He considers himself too unworthy
to accept praise even when someone else offers it.

Believe in yourself. Affirm, "I am intelligent. I am
creative. I am involved." Everyone has some degree
of intelligence and creativity. Psychiatrists today know
that child prodigies are not born—they are developed.
It's a phenomenon in human development, for it
means that the child who scores the lowest grades is
really a potential genius. Only the person who respects,
esteems and values himself is going to get involved
and use his abilities.

I am somebody because I am a child of God!

Enthusiasm for Life—Here's How

"Then he said to all, 'Anyone who wants to follow me must put aside his own desires and conveniences and carry his cross with him every day and keep close to me!'"

Luke 9:23

Shouldering your cross means to make a commitment! When you get involved, you discover people are hurting. When you make a commitment, you stick with a problem until it becomes a possibility!

A newspaper ad exposed the "in" fashions and trends in America. At that time designer jeans were "out," and Levis were "in." Certain restaurants were passe, and others were becoming popular. Tennis and racquetball were "out," and golf was coming back. The article surveyed the cities and lifestyles of the United States. One item excited me. Living together before marriage is "out," and marriage is "in." Isn't it nice to know commitment is back "in."

The teachings of Jesus are eternal. They may go in and out of fashion, but His truths will always rise to the surface.

**Jesus is the same yesterday,
today and tomorrow.**

Enthusiasm for Life—Here's How

"If you love your life down here—you will lose it. If you despise your life down here—you will exchange it for eternal glory."

John 12:25

When you make a commitment, you assume a cross. To pay a price means your ego is on the line. To run the risk of failure is to attempt to do something great.

I learned years ago that I'd rather attempt to do something great and fail, than to attempt to do nothing and succeed. Yet most people are afraid of commitments. An innate fear exists in most of us. The fear of having an ego blowout at high speed in heavy traffic. Or embarrassment! Commitment means being willing to be embarrassed, to pay the price, and to carry the cross.

What commitment would you make today if you knew it could not fail? If you are willing to be committed to something great, here's what will happen. Commitment will produce energy. Energy will produce enthusiasm. Enthusiasm will produce a whole new way of living!

The cross is the key to enthusiasm.

Enthusiasm for Life—Here's How

*"For anyone who keeps his life for himself shall lose it; and
anyone who loses his life for me shall find it again."*
                                                    Matthew 16:25

In his book, *There's a Lot More to Health than Not Being
Sick,* Bruce Larson tells the story of an old woman who died
in a nursing home in Scotland. She left nothing of monetary
value, but in going through her only possessions, a nurse
found the following poem which the old woman had written.

What do you see, nurses, what do you see?
What are you thinking when you're looking at me?
A crabby old woman not very wise,
Uncertain of habit with faraway eyes.
I'm a small child of ten with a mother and father,
Brothers and sisters who love one another,
A bride in her twenties—my heart gives a leap.
Remembering the vow that I promised to keep.
A woman of thirty, my young now grow fast,
Bound to each other with ties that should last.
At forty, my sons have grown and have gone,
But my man is beside me, to see I don't mourn.
At fifty, once more babies play around my knees;
Again we know children, my husband and me.
I'm an old woman now and nature is cruel;
'Tis her jest to make old age look like a fool.
The body it crumbles, grace and vigor depart;
There is now a stone where I once had a heart.
But inside this old carcass a young girl still dwells,
And now and again my battered heart swells.
I remember the joys, and I remember the pain;
And I am loving and living life over again.
I think of the years all too few—gone too fast,
And accept the stark fact that nothing can last.
So open your eyes, nurses, open and see
Not a crabbed old woman; look closer—see me.

Commitment turns weights into wings!

Enthusiasm for Life—Here's How

*"What profit is there if you gain the whole world—
and lose eternal life? What can be compared with
the value of eternal life?"*

                                        Matthew 16:26

Involvement, commitment, and *follow-through.*
That's what Jesus did. Look at His life. He had a
positive self-image. He never put himself down,
because He had self-esteem. His commitment was
a cross. He followed through—to the resurrection!
Eternal life!

For years I have worn the Possibility Thinker's
medallion. Inscribed on the back are the words of
the Possibility Thinker's Creed:

When faced with a mountain, I will not quit.
I will keep on striving until I climb over,
find a pass through, tunnel underneath,
or simply stay and turn the mountain into
a gold mine with God's help."

Affirm today that Jesus can use you. Believe
that you can spread His love around. Be willing
to become involved in your world. Then make a
commitment to let Christ's love flow through you.
Finally, follow-through, and let Him be the Lord
of your life.

**Jesus, you are the Lord of my life.
Love others through me.**

TRY GOD AND
TUNE INTO LIFE

Try Trusting the God Who Loves You

"He said to him, 'You shall love the Lord your God with your whole heart, with your whole soul, and with your whole mind. This is the great and chief commandment. The second is like it, You shall love your neighbor as yourself. On these two commandments, the whole Law and the Prophets depend.'"

Matthew 22:37-40

I'm excited to have the opportunity to share a faith that unites many faiths. Many people think that the family of God is divided and fighting among itself: Catholics against Jews; Protestants against Catholics; Jews against Protestants. That's not true!

Here's a story a Roman Catholic friend told me recently: "Every day in going to the office, I ride the elevator with a friend," he said. "He's Jewish and I'm Catholic. Naturally, I was surprised one day when on the way up in the elevator he made the sign of the cross. 'Aaron,' I said, 'I thought you were Jewish?' He answered, 'I am.' I asked, 'Then why did you make the sign of the cross?' 'Oh,' he replied, 'I didn't—I was just checking my tie, my belt, and my collar.'

"This story is true," remarked my friend, "and the reason why Aaron and I get along so well is because we have a common bond. We both live by the Ten Commandments."

There is nothing as powerful as positive religion. Real faith releases energy and energy is health!

Real faith releases energy

Try Trusting the God Who Loves You

"One who has clean hands and a pure heart, who has not lifted their soul to falsehood, who has not sworn deceptively; shall receive a blessing from the Lord, and righteousness from the God of salvation."

Psalm 24:4-5

What do body chemicals have to do with the Ten Commandments? Everything! For the Ten Commandments are ten positive prescriptions, not ten negative restrictions! They are ten tips on how to really enjoy life to the fullest.

At the deepest level, what really makes you enjoy life? It's not the sensation of the moment. No. It's the sense that you have acquired character and class. It's knowing you've developed qualities as a human being which allow you to have self-respect, self-dignity and self-esteem.

When you feel good about yourself, then you can really enjoy life

Try Trusting the God Who Loves You

"When you become a Christian you become a brand new person inside. You are not the same anymore. A new life has begun!"
                                    II Corinthians 5:17

The real key to personal pride, self-dignity and self-respect is found in successful relationships. That's where a dynamic, positive religion comes in. True, Christianity is not a set of rituals. To some people in some churches, religion is nothing more than a game. They read the Bible, offer prayers, sing songs, take up an offering, listen to a sermon, say a benediction and leave. It's a Sunday morning ritual.

For others, religion is nothing more than a set of regulations. It's a life of do's and don'ts. To others, it's a matter of restrictions—a negative force to keep you from really enjoying life.

Real religion is not regulations, rituals or restrictions. Real religion is a relationship!

Real Christianity roots itself in a personal relationship to Jesus Christ!

Thank you, God that I can have a relationship with You through your Son

Try Trusting the God Who Loves You

"You shall have no other gods before me."
                                        Exodus 20:3

If you really want to feel good about yourself, follow the Ten Commandments. The first one says, "Thou shalt have no other gods before me." In other words, God is the kind of God who can really help you. He alone can give you what you really need.

The problem in the world today is not an absence of religion. Human beings, whether they know it or not, are incurably, irretrievably, non-negotiably religious. What do I mean? I mean they're insecure. All of us are. What's insecurity? I'll answer with a question. What is it that tells a salmon where to go? It's born, swims down to the ocean and somehow knows when and where to swim upstream by the way of the right river to find the place where it was born. No one knows what guides the salmon back.

Insecurity is an emotion which God instilled within us to draw us back to Him. In the search for solutions to insecurities, humans have managed to create many gods. My warning is this: make sure you are trusting the right God!

Trust the God who loves you!

Try Trusting the God Who Loves You

".....Jesus said, 'My time has come; the glory of God will soon surround me—and God shall receive great praise because of all that happens to me.'"

John 13:31

One of the modern gods is Stateism. If you trust government to take care of you, the collective power of the political system then becomes the representation of a god-almightly. The trouble with that type of god is you soon lose your freedom. That god doesn't love you.

Another god offered today is one I label Scientism. With all the greatest respect for scientists, I admit I've often seen them become the white gods in society. Scientism becomes a replacement for God when it steps out of its natural role and tries to answer all the questions.

Secularism is another popular god. That's the human potential movement that says you can do anything you want to do by yourself. No one believes in possibility thinking and motivation more than I do, yet I'm not a secularist. I don't believe you can do anything you want by yourself. You need Divine Guidance from a true God.

The true God is not the god of stateism, scientism, or secularism. The true God is the Savior's God. It is the God that Jesus Christ believed in.

I need the divine guidance of the true God

Try Trusting the God Who Loves You

"He delivered us from so deadly a peril, and He will deliver us; on Him we have set our hope that He will deliver us again."

II Corinthians 1:10

Allan Phillips was driving through the 11,665 foot high Grenally Pass in Colorado on January 6, 1982. An unforecasted storm struck, and he found himself in a blizzard, stuck. Roads were closed. He was completely alone with no hope of rescue as darkness fell. He didn't even have enough gas to keep his car running until morning.

He knew he would freeze to death. Suddenly, an idea came into his mind. He would signal for help with his headlights using Morse Code. Out of simple faith, he signaled for help.

An airplane was overhead. A passenger who knew Morse Code looked out the window and thought he saw something. He went to the pilot. "I think I've seen a Morse Code—an SOS signal." The pilot radioed the FAA and two snow plows were sent to rescue Allan Phillips.

There is a lot in the spiritual universe that we don't understand. But we have a God who cares and who guides.

Our God guides us through the storm

Try Trusting the God Who Loves You

"Let your conduct be free from the love of money. Be satisfied with what you have, for He has said, 'I will not give you up nor desert you.'"
                                        Hebrews 13:5

My father never used to say anything. He was the quietest man I know. All through my childhood, my mother and father had a good marriage. But they had their problems. My mother would get upset with my dad and say, "Why don't you say something? Why don't you talk?" He'd reply, "What should I say?" And my mother would say, "Anything—just something!"

When my father died, I'll never forget how much my mother missed him. "But he never said anything," I said to her one day. "How can you miss him so much?" But she answered me, "Oh, I just always knew he was there."

Trust the God who's always there. Trust the God who loves you. Discover what a beautiful human being you can become. Discover how to feel really good about yourself.

Trust the God who's always there

Try True Faith—It Works Wonders

"In the beginning God created the heaven and the earth."

Genesis 1:1

The Ten Commandments are the foundation of the Jewish and Christian faiths—ten universal principles designed not as negative restrictions but the divine prescriptions which reveal how to really enjoy life and feel good about ourselves.

The second commandment states, "Make no graven images of God." In other words, be sure the image you have of God is correct. What is God really like? The atheist says He does not exist. The agnostic says He can't be understood. But the evidence of His existence is overwhelming. Walk into a building like the Crystal Cathedral and you must assume there was an architect; walk across a wet beach and see footprints in the sand and you must assume someone else had been there. Walk in the desert and find rocks of equal size piled on ten neat pyramids and you must assume someone had organized them that way.

In the same way, the most brilliant scientists look at our universe and sense God's scheme in the whole system. They may not understand who God is and thus call themselves agnostics, but they can't ignore His existence.

Ultimately, to know God depends upon revelation. God has to let us know who He is.

Thank you, God, for showing me who You are

Try True Faith—It Works Wonders

"You shall not make for yourself any graven image, or any likeness of anything that is in heaven above, or that is in the earth beneath, or that is in the water under the earth."

Exodus 20:5

The human being is intuitively religious. Long before the Ten Commandments were written, people were religious. But not knowing God, they made graven images. They had to imagine what God was like. Throughout history, the worst and the best behavior has happened in the name of religion. Why? Because some of the worst people had the wrong image of God.

What are some of the wrong images of God? One false view of God is that of God-the-Grand-Patriarch. This view perceives God like Santa Claus, a wonderful old grandfather—gentle, good, giving whatever we need or want. Yet the Bible does not present Him like this.

"The Bible presents God as a loving father, one who knows the very best for his children...

A Father who is not afraid to rebuke a child if he knows the child will grow stronger through his positive and constructive criticisms.

Let's have the right image of God

Try True Faith—It Works Wonders

"Everything has been handed over to Me from My Father, and no one really knows the Son except the Father, nor does anyone understand the Father except the Son and he or she to whom the Son wishes to reveal Him."

Matthew 11:27

One of the funniest things I ever saw happened this past Christmas. At a self-serve gas station, pumping gas into his car, was a full bearded Santa Claus. Upon finishing his task, he proceeded to pay by credit card! When Santa operates on credit, then we're really in trouble!

Seriously, the problem is, too many people are taught as children that there is a Santa Claus at the same time they are taught about God. With their child's understanding, they can't make the necessary distinction. When they finally realize there is no Santa Claus, they suppose there is no God either. If there is a God—perhaps he's like Santa Claus.

If God isn't a glorified Santa, what is He? The true image of God is much more glorious than we imagine. God Himself is the reality of Jesus Christ. He came from heaven to tell us the truth about God.

Jesus Christ is God and He loved us enough to come down from heaven to reveal Himself to us

Try True Faith—It Works Wonders

"But do not overlook this one fact, dear friends, that with the Lord one day is as a thousand years and a thousand years as one day."
                                        II Peter 3:8

I don't feel it's a coincidence that the order of creation revealed in Genesis is precisely that of the process of evolution. This leaves for no conflict at all—unless you hold to the belief that the days recorded in the Scriptures indicate a twenty-four hour period as we now know them. Many Evangelical Christians don't believe the days were twenty-four hour period of time. How could they be when there was no sun or light for the first few days?

I suspect God created the universe in millions, billions of years. Don't perceive God is so small that He must fit into a mold. God is bigger than that. It's easy to have a false image of God. No wonder, intelligent people often become agnostics.

The danger is that many end up denying the existence of God simply because He doesn't fit into their preconceived notions of what they believe he should be.

God is too big to fit into my mold

Try True Faith—It Works Wonders

"I and my Father are one."

John 10:30

What can we believe about God? Take a close look at Jesus Christ. God is a God of love. Christ made that clear. God is also a God who works through human thought and emotion. That's why possibility thinking is a theology of health and wholeness and has its roots in the full Gospel of Jesus Christ. When you get the right image of God, He will change your life. He'll show you possibilities. He'll develop your untapped potential.

The key is when Christ comes into your life. When that happens, your life becomes what you never, ever, expected it to be!

The Bible tells us that we are made in the very image of God—so hold on!—and be prepared to move into new areas of living.

Expect the best when you look up to God.

Jesus, come into my life and make it like a window for your love to shine through

Try True Faith—It Works Wonders

"I have been crucified with Christ; I no longer live as myself, but Christ lives within me; the life I now live in the flesh I live by faith in the Son of God, who loved me and gave Himself for me."
Galatians 2:20

Yours can be a life like Dorothy Gossage. She died recently, leaving behind the memory of a great life to all who knew her. At age fifteen, Dorothy was an athletic young cheerleader when she was given injections to cure mild arthritis. Instead of curing her, they paralyzed her. She could move nothing but her eyes and lips.

One day she looked at the crucifix of Christ on her wall. She prayed, "Jesus, if it's possible, can you come off the cross and enter my life?" She felt a tingle in her thumb, and tried to bend it; her entire arm rose until her thumb brushed her cheek. She screamed, "I moved my arm! Jesus is alive!"

Dorothy married a widower and adopted his sixteen children. At his death she had to support the children, so she started her own business—a telephone answering service. It became one of the most successful job placement services in the county, and she credited it to her living God—not a carved sculpture, but a strong spirit, the reality of Jesus Christ in her life.

If you want to truly know God, don't look at an image. Look at Jesus Christ.

Try Taking God Seriously

*"And no one can ever lay any other real founda-
tion than that one we already have—Jesus Christ."*
I Corinthians 3:11

I believe the Ten Commandments are the
underground foundation stones upon which the
whole philosophy of possibility thinking rests.
Possibility thinking isn't the brainchild of Robert
Schuller. It comes from the Old Testament and
the New Testament climaxed by Jesus Himself.
And the foundation stones are the Ten Commandments. You probably don't see them and think
about them, but they're there. And if they weren't
there, the whole faith would collapse.

It's like the Crystal Cathedral. To some it may
look so fragile, so ethereal, so gossamer. Like a
spider web of steel and a sheet of glass. How could
it stand under an earthquake? It has withstood two
already. How can it stand the strong winds? It has.
Why? Because underneath there are foundations.
Three hundred nineteen concrete roots that go
down forty five feet into the ground. The Ten
Commandments are the deep pillars on which our
faith is built.

**I will stand firm through the winds
on the basis of my faith**

Try Taking God Seriously

"The Lord will hear when I call to Him."
                              Psalm 4:3

The third Commandment says, "Thou shalt not take the name of the Lord thy God in vain." Now let me put that very positively. What does it mean? It means this: God wants you to take Him so seriously that you will pray to Him, talk to Him, then listen to Him. He tells us to call upon His name and He will answer us.

Jesus Christ taught the Lord's Prayer. It's really built on the third commandment. "Our Father, Who art in heaven, hallowed be Thy Name, Thy Kingdom come, Thy will be done on earth as it is in Heaven." The entire Lord's Prayer is really built as an extension to the positive fulfillment of the third commandment.

One of the greatest dangers I believe Americans have to deal with is an attitude of taking things for granted. You'll never totally appreciate your freedoms until you understand or experience the confinement of the Communist world.

In the same way, be careful not to take God for-granted either.

Take him seriously, as his word asks.

**I'll call upon God and know
He will answer me**

Try Taking God Seriously

"You shall not take the name of the Lord your God in vain; for the Lord will not hold him guiltless who takes His name in vain."

Exodus 20:7

God cannot guarantee that you will have a strong self image if you don't have a strong prayerful relationship with Him. "Thou will not hold him guiltless who takes His name in vain." What does it mean? That means that God cannot guarantee you that you're going to feel good about yourself and have a strong sense of self worth if you don't maintain a close relationship with Him at all times. What God is saying here is that if you take Him seriously and learn how to pray positively, unbelievable miracles happen.

**I will learn how to pray
positively and continuously**

Try Taking God Seriously

"Be glad for all God is planning for you. Be patient in trouble, and prayerful always."
Romans 12:12

Carol Lovell was at work when she was robbed and had five bullets fired into her brain. All through six hours of surgery and a long, slow recovery, Carol decided to remain calm and alive. She said, "When you lose your calm and nerve, you lose your head and then you lose everything. And I certainly wanted to live."

Carol walks by herself today! She talks! Her only limitation is a slightly handicapped hand. There are mysterious, magnificent, marvelous powers that God has built into the brain that release incredible chemicals for healing and health. If you call upon His name, not in vain but in truth!

If you keep this commandment, you'll know that there's a God who puts you in this world and He's got a beautiful plan for your life, and a bullet can be lodged in your brain and you can still be a walking miracle.

God has a beautiful plan for my life

Try Taking God Seriously

"No distrust made him waver concerning the promise of God, but he grew strong in his faith as he gave glory to God, fully convinced that God was able to do what He had promised."
                                        Romans 4:20-21

Lucille Hampton is an award winning sculptress. Some time ago, she was flat on her back from an injury from which she was not expected to recover. Somebody gave her a thirty cent piece of clay one day. As she lay in her bed, she pulled a bobby pin from her hair and started playing with that piece of clay, following an inner impulse. That piece of clay, formed with a hairpin, turned into a piece of sculpture that she sold for $2,500.00! And her career was off and flying.

Thou shalt not take the name of the Lord thy God in vain—you had better take God seriously and begin to believe in the dreams He puts into your mind. You are taking God's name in vain if you don't take seriously the opportunities and challenges He gives to you.

**I will believe God's dreams—
I will accept His challenges**

Try Taking God Seriously

"But Moses said to God, 'Who am I that I should go to Pharoah, and bring the sons of Israel out of Egypt?' God said, 'But I will be with you....'"
Exodus 3:11-12

How do you take God's name seriously? You listen to Him. He is speaking to you and to me every minute of every hour of every day. How does He speak to us? Sometimes, of course, in the still, quiet times. Sometimes God speaks to us through warnings. He speaks to us through invitations, through encouragement, through promises. He speaks to us through inner visions, those impossible dreams. When He speaks, do not take His name in vain. Don't brush Him off and say it's impossible.

**I will trust God and believe
His dreams are possible**

Try Taking God Seriously

"And my spirit hath rejoiced in God my Savior."
                                        Luke 1:47

The people who break the third commandment are the people who don't take God seriously. When He calls you to do something, to be someone, do you dare take the risk? Do you dare take a chance? Do you dare to believe it could happen? Jesus Christ, we Christians believe, is alive! We believe He's come into this world to be an inspiration, a still, small voice, a Saviour, and a friend. What dream do you have today?

Jesus Christ is my Saviour and Friend

Try Taking God Seriously

"Mary Magdalene came, bringing the disciples news, 'I have seen the Lord and He told me this.'"
John 20:18

Dr. Irwin J. Lubbers was the president of Hope College in my undergraduate days. Years ago, he and his young son, Aaron, were taking a trip when icy roads flipped their car over into a ditch. Dr. Lubbers lost consciousness and wondered if he would survive.

He awoke and found himself being held up in the arms of his little boy, who was crying and praying, "Dear Jesus, please don't let my Daddy die." Next to his son, Dr. Lubbers saw clearly the Lord Jesus Christ. He wanted to rush to Him and stay with Him forever. But his son begged him to stay.

In telling this story, Dr. Lubbers said, "The skeptics can say what they want. I don't care. I am an educator, a rationalist, a scientist, and I know I saw the Lord. He's alive!"

If we take God seriously, then we believe that Jesus Christ is alive—and available to us.

Jesus my Lord is alive!

Try Taking God Seriously

"Ask, and it shall be given you; seek, and ye shall find; knock, and it shall be opened unto you.
　　　　　　　　　　　Matthew 7:7

There is a God. Believe in Him. You can call to Him and He will answer. You will pray and He will hear. What do you need—guidance? Ask for it. He'll give it. Courage? Ask for it. He'll give it. Forgiveness of sins? Ask for it. He'll give it. What do you need? Hope? He will give it, if you take His name seriously. Now.

**God will give me what I need when
I take His name seriously**

Try Taking God Seriously

"Yet it was because of this that God raised Him up to the heights of heaven and gave Him a name which is above every other name."
Philippians 2:9

Thank you, God, that you've given us the foundation stones of possibility thinking faith. Truly Your Name is wonderful. Someone now, O Lord, reading this message is having a change of heart. They are being converted to Christianity. Suddenly, Lord, at a deep level, their lives are being redeemed. Thank you, God. Forgive us for the times we didn't take Your name seriously and we let the ideas fly right by. We accept you now, Jesus Christ. You lived, You died, You rose again. You are alive today! You are our Friend. You are the Name above all names and we honor Your Name by claiming You as our Savior.

Amen

**Jesus has redeemed me—
He is my savior**

Try God's Way to Creative Communications

"Therefore comfort one another with these words."

I Thessalonians 4:18

"Thou shalt not take the name of the Lord thy God in vain." This is an invitation to discover the power that positive language can have in daily life.

Words have within them the power to release either positive or negative emotions. What this Commandment urges us to do is to discover the language and vocabulary that will elevate our sense of self-esteem, self-worth and self-dignity. It is amazing what language can do to the collective self esteem of a whole society. When the language in a culture is positive, it can raise the level of self dignity. When it's negative, it can demean an entire generation.

**Positive language can elevate
my self esteem**

Try God's Way to Creative Communications

"Follow the pattern of the sound words which you have heard from me, in the faith and love which are in Christ Jesus."

II Timothy 1:13

I appeal to you—let's commit ourselves to a disciplined vocabulary where we not only build our own self esteem but raise the level of self esteem in our society. It is extremely important that we become educated and informed in the use of positive words that can achieve positive results.

I have a friend, Harv Hoffman. I remember his telling the story of when he went out with his wife during the depression and, because they didn't have the money to buy anything, often would go out to window shop. One night he was looking in a jewelry store, and his wife saw a beautiful bracelet and said, "Harv, I really would like it. Don't you think you could buy it for me?" Now Harv has a masterful use of words, and he replied, "Honey, extenuating circumstances perforce me to preclude you from such a multiple extravagance." She said, "I don't get it." And he answered, "That's just what I said."

We can use words to build up or to tear down, to create emotions of unspeakable beauty or feelings of utmost degradation. Like my friend, Harv, we should choose our words carefully, finding ways to express even the negative in positive terms.

I will commit myself to a disciplined vocabulary

Try God's Way to Creative Communications

"She opens her mouth with wisdom, and the teaching of kindness is on her tongue."
                                    Proverbs 31:26

Somebody said that profanity is the clumsy effort of a feeble mind to express itself forcibly. I think of all the English speaking societies, we have to take our hats off to the British in knowing how to use the English language effectively. The English have had a tradition for noble carriage, a dignified manner, cultivated and cultured moods, and part of this is attributed to the language.

Like the English, I think we should cut our use of words down. We need to develop an economy of words. I am reminded of Disraeli's comment about Gladstone. Gladstone was such a long winded politician, you know, and Disraeli said, "The trouble with Gladstone is he's intoxicated by the exuberance of his own verbosity." The English have had such a command of the language that they can even insult people without insulting them.

It takes wisdom and wit to come up with creative ways to handle negative feelings or situations. Profanity, on the other hand, requires no forethought. It tumbles out of the mouth quickly, bringing with it injured feelings and broken relationships.

I will develop an economy of words and learn to use English effectively

Try God's Way to Creative Communication

*"A fool gives full vent to anger, but the wise
person, holding it back, quiets it."*
                                    Proverbs 29:11

There is a great potential power of feeling good
and achieving success if we can learn to use and
utilize the power of words positively, not negatively. Classically, the third commandment has
been thought to mean, "Do not use profanity." Is
anything wrong with profanity? Why, of course.
Profanity demeans the human race. And some
words are offensive, which means that somebody's
dignity is insulted and lowered by someone's
choice of words.

There was a bus driver in Chicago who had a
female passenger who was really irritated by
something. She let loose with a string of unrepeat-
able words. Everybody was ashamed. And then
the bus stopped; the profane passenger got ready
to disembark, and the bus driver said, "Madame,
you left something behind." She shot him a defiant
glance and asked what it was. He answered, "A
very bad impression."

**Use words positively and see
how good it feels**

Try God's Way to Creative Communication

*"Anyone who says he or she is a Christian but
doesn't control their sharp tongue is just fooling
themselves, and their religion isn't worth much."*
                                        James 1:26

How do you handle anger? How do you handle
temper? How do you handle upsetting experiences? The normal negative reaction is to just let
go with some profane language, of course. The
third commandment is an invitation to cultivate a
skillful, sophisticated capacity to handle upsetting
experiences with calmness and with equanimity.
Utilize the powerful force of words positively
instead of negatively, because any time a negative
experience attacks you, you have the freedom to
choose how you will react.

When you react with words that contribute to
the collectivized lower level of self esteem in your
community, you become part of the very problem
that you were swearing at two minutes ago.

**I have the freedom to choose to react to
upsetting experiences in a positive way**

Try God's Way to Creative Communication

"The tongue of the righteous is choice silver."
Proverbs 10:20

You can choose how you will react to any situation and you can choose your own vocabulary. What kind of words do you use? Every word stimulates an emotion. A word is not just an accumulation of letters to form a verbal symbol. It's more than that. A word is an encapsulation of an emotion. Words release energy, either positive or negative. A word can either turn you on or turn you off. If it's positive, it releases positive energy and becomes a literal creative force.

When God created the world, what tool did He use? His tongue. He spoke a word that was creative energy. He said, "Let there be light." And there was light. "Let the dry land separate from the waters." Separation occurred. Whether that is literally true or allegorical, this is the truth: Words can release energy or words can absorb energy.

You can energize your own life and lives around you through the communication of positive and uplifting words!

Let me speak so that my words release positive, creative energy

Try God's Way to Creative Communication

*"Death and life are in the power of the tongue,
and those who love it will eat its fruit."*
                                        Proverbs 18:21

Have you ever been in a committee meeting,
when someone gets a creative idea? People are
excited, energy is flowing, until someone
arrogantly declares, "Look, what you are
proposing is utterly impossible." The energy
drains away and the creative force is dissipated.

Words are powerful things. The third commandment is violated, God's name is dishonored,
anytime we reduce peoples' pride and dignity
by using words that will cut them down, embarrass
them, humiliate them, or strip them of their pride.
We need to go through the discipline of sifting
negative words from positive words.

**God, give me the discipline to sift negative
words and eliminate them
from my vocabulary**

Try God's Way to Creative Communication

"Better is a poor one who walks in integrity than one who is perverse in speech, and is a fool."

Proverbs 19:1

The other day my wife and I were invited out to breakfast. It was held in a beautiful, elegant dining room. We noticed a very distinguished gentleman who came and sat in the booth next to us. He was elegantly dressed—everything about his attire made him stand out as an impeccable gentleman. He was barely seated when he uttered a sentence that included about five words which I can only describe as the kind of language an angry farmer wouldn't use in the barnyard. His style of dress and his bearing contradicted the words that came from his mouth. Suddenly, he was no longer a gentleman. He demeaned himself; robbed himself of dignity. All his noble bearing, his elegant manner,were wiped out in one careless, crude sentence.

I invite you today to make a decision to help turn the tide in America. I'd like to believe it's not too late to save the English language. Let's make a commitment to really live first class, elegant and dignified lives. Let's start by learning to speak English, choosing the kind of words that bring pride to ourselves and to those around us.

The self esteem of America starts with me and the kinds of words I choose to speak

SUCCESS—IT'S YOURS
FOR THE ASKING!

Self Esteem...The Need for Success

"So I pray for you . . . that God who gives you hope will keep you happy and full of peace as you believe in him!"

Romans 15:13

Some people think it is materialistic of me to talk about success. But I believe we *need* to feel successful!

Dr. Bertram Brown, Director of the National Institute for Mental Health, said that mental depression costs the United States $5 billion a year! This astronomical cost is related to *indirect* hospital and drug expenses, and does not even include the direct costs attributed to suicides and those in mental hospitals who are supported by our taxes. Suicide is the third cause of death among teenagers, and eleventh among Americans in general. Interestingly, the leading profession in suicides is the psychiatric profession.

Dr. Brown was asked if a depressed person had to seek professional help or was there something he could do for himself. He answered that a person could do a great deal to lift his own depression. But he felt the most important concept was to build into yourself the idea that you are not helpless or hopeless. Give yourself the opportunity for successful experiences to counteract feelings of helplessness. We *need* success!

My mind is filled with thoughts of you, Lord, and I am filled with joy!

Self Esteem...The Need for Success

"Let this mind be in you, which was also in Christ Jesus."

Philippians 2:5

Let's face it, we all make mistakes. I've had my failures, and you've had yours. Failures come when we get life's messages mixed up.

A florist was asked to send flowers to a newly-married couple who were moving into their new home. The florist also had an order to send flowers for a funeral. Well, he got the cards mixed up! The newlyweds received the message, "Our deepest sympathy to both of you." At the funeral, they received the message, "Good luck in your new location." Needless to say, if the florist continues crossing his messages, he'll be out of business before long.

Living beyond the possibility of personal failure (and avoiding mistakes) means to succeed. Somerset Maugham once said, "There's a common idea that success spoils people by making them vain and egotistical; but actually this is erroneous. On the contrary, it makes people for the most part humble, tolerant and gentle. It is failure that makes people bitter and cruel." We need to experience success. We need to unmix life's messages, and plan for success in our lives.

**My mind is clear and available
for God's power!**

Self Esteem...The Need for Success

"Jesus Christ is the same yesterday, today, and forever."

Hebrews 13:8

The secret of success is to find a need and fill it, and Jesus Christ does that! What are these profound, classical, non-fashionable needs that He meets?

Sigmund Freud said the will to pleasure or sensuality is the primary stimulus of the human life. Sensuality is a profound need; and according to Freud, the ultimate need.

Another psychologist picked up where Freud left off. Adler believed that the will to power was greater than the will to pleasure. The need to be in control and up at bat is the deepest need, he claimed.

Viktor Frankl, a highly-acclaimed psychologist today, stated that the deepest human need is to see meaning in what you are doing. To live a day of life and see no meaning or purpose in it would be terrible! Like the man who said that life is so meaningless it's like sticking your finger in the bucket of water and pulling it out again; there is no hole left afterward! "I feel I could die today," he said, "and nobody would miss me."

We are saved from such emptiness through Jesus Christ Who not only gives our life meaning and purpose, but also identity!

I am one with Christ!

Self Esteem...The Need for Success

"So God made man like his Maker. Like God did God make man; Man and maid did he make them."

Genesis 1:27

I once said to Dr. Viktor Frankl, "Even meaning is meaningless unless it feeds my self-esteem because the deepest need of a human being is self-esteem."

Deeper than sensuality, deeper than status or power, deeper than significance is self-esteem. I have to feel like I am worth something, and so do you. Don't let people put you down and say you're on an ego trip. If a person has no ego needs, that person is sick. The ego needs stem from our deepest need to feel worthy, and Jesus Christ does this. That's why He's still the most popular person in the world today!

Someone at the Los Angeles Airport once asked a cab driver to take him to Christ's Church. The cab driver took him all the way to Orange County and dropped him off at the Crystal Cathedral. The passenger said that he wanted Christ's Church, and the cab driver said, "If He's in town, He'll be here!"

**Because I have self-love,
I have self-worth.**

Love…The Creed for Success

"But the person who truly loves God is the one who is open to God's knowledge."
I Corinthians 8:3

The dogma, doctrine, law, universal principle, non-negotiable, beyond compromise, like-gravity-itself creed for success is *love*!

A young boy once asked a wealthy man, "How can I become successful like you when I grow up?" The man answered that first, you've got to fall in love with yourself! Second, you've got to fall in love with people! And third, you've got to fall in love with life!

He continued, "Be thankful for whatever job you have. Be thankful for your boss. Be thankful for your fellow employees. Be the first one to arrive and the last one to leave; except for coffee breaks, then be the last one to leave and the first one to return. And wear a red shirt so you'll stand out!"

Don't be afraid to show your love. Display your gratitude. And be interested in doing a job well. If you do these things, you won't need to look for success; it will find *you*.

**God's power within me gives me
the courage to show love!**

Love...The Creed for Success

"All the special gifts and powers from God will someday come to an end, but love goes on forever."

I Corinthians 13:8

Jesus Christ is still the most successful person Who ever lived, because He makes me feel like I am somebody!

When President Gerald Ford was on Hour of Power, I told him I had never been invited into the oval office at the White House. And I teased, "Why don't you run for president again, get elected and invite me to the oval office?" If I were invited, I think I might appear to be on an ego trip. I'd really feel like I was somebody! Or if the President of the United States visited my home, I'd really feel important! When President Ford worships with us, we all feel more important, don't we? As Americans, we are honored when he comes for a visit.

But when Jesus Christ came to visit the human race, He gave us our greatest honor. By His incarnation, He honored the human race. By His crucifixion, He put a value on us. And by his resurrection, He took early retirement and gave us His job to spread love around the world. If you don't feel you're important, all you have to do is get invited to the private office of the Lord Himself! And that's easy, you just ask Him.

Jesus Christ has made me valuable!

Love...The Creed for Success

"Be gentle and ready to forgive; never hold grudges. Remember, the Lord forgave you, so you must forgive others."

Colossians 3:13

Jesus Christ loves you and wants to live in your life. When you let Him, your first experience will be genuine pardon. The most beautiful word in the world is pardon. It means I forgive you even though you don't deserve it. If you deserved it, it would be a fair deal, not pardon.

That is a profound theological concept some people can't handle. Those who are so hung up on justice they have no room for mercy are the losers. When we are forgiven, we are liberated to really love. Interpersonal relationships bring disappointments and the temptation to resent the person who caused the problem. But, if you have had the experience of unconditional, non-judgmental love, of being forgiven *anyway*, in spite of what you've done, that changes your life! Jesus does not love you "if," He loves you *anyway!*

My anger and resentments are slipping away as I thank God for His forgiveness!

Love...The Creed for Success

"But as for me, I will come into your Temple protected by your mercy and your love; I will worship you with deepest awe."

Psalm 5:7

The unconditional pardon of Christ produces poise. The tension of subconscious guilt is removed. Some people call this experience being "born again," and it's true! Life changes drastically when you know that you and God are good friends. Poise enables you to cope. It gives you power, the kind of power to hang in there forever!

You can be a person into whose life the love of Jesus Christ pours. In a world like ours today, we just can't have too much genuine love. Yet, you can't love until you've been forgiven. When you fully grasp that pardon, you'll feel clean! God lifts the load from us. The black pages are torn and thrown away. The stains are removed. The cuts are healed. Accept His forgiveness today, and let your life reflect His love and forgiveness to others.

If God has chosen me for His friend, I must be a marvelous person. I am!

Love...The Creed for Success

"But make everyone rejoice who puts his trust in you. Keep them shouting for joy because you are defending them. Fill all who love you with your happiness."

Psalm 34:17

What causes love to blossom in a life? It's certainly not human nature. By nature we tend to be insecure, defensive, highly protective. We wear masks to create an impression so people will like us. To inflate our image, we join the right clubs, and end up doing all kinds of weird things in a feeble attempt to attain a level of importance.

By nature, every human being has problems with his own self-image. Nobody really has the respect for himself he ought to. Every person puts himself down too much. I've never met a person who loves himself as much as God loves him. Nor have I met someone who would sacrifice his son on a cross for another's soul. Yet, God did that for us!

If a person doesn't love himself, he's too empty of love to give it away; too unworthy of it, he thinks to accept it. Yet through Jesus Christ we are reborn. We attain importance because of Him. After all, there's no one in a higher position than our God. He fills us with His love! He fills our deepest emptiness. He is more than sufficient! How grateful we can be to Him for his all-encompassing love for us!

Jesus Christ has made me important!

Love...The Creed for Success

"But God showed his great love for us by sending Christ to die for us while we were still sinners."
Romans 5:8

Forgiveness is non-judgmental love. I recall the doctor who spoke at the World Psychiatric Congress on the value of love. He told us the only real love is a non-judgmental love.

Most people love judgmentally: I'll love you if you agree with me politically. I'll love you if you'll start living a cleaner life. If you don't meet my expectations, I will not love you.

But St. Paul tells us that even when we were the enemies of God, He loves us non-judgmentally. There are no "ifs" in God's love for us!

In the Sermon on the Mount, Jesus said that if we love only those who agree with us, what is so great about that? Even scoundrels and crooks love their fellow crooks. Genuine love is shown when God allows the sun to shine on the just and the unjust, and His rain falls on the good as well as the evil.

That may seem unjust to you, but this concept is filled with mercy. There will always be a tension between mercy and justice! If you are having difficulty forgiving someone because "what they did is just not right," let me encourage you to forgive as you have been forgiven.

I am forgiven:
therefore, I am forgiving!

Love...The Creed for Success

"Don't repay evil for evil. Don't snap back at those who say unkind things about you. Instead, pray for God's help for them. For we are to be kind to others, and God will bless us for it."
                                                    I Peter 3:9

As a boy, I loved the winter snows. But what we didn't appreciate were the blizzards, because they would come in with driving winds of 50 to 60 miles an hour and close the roads. We would be isolated on our farm. The only good thing about the blizzard was that I didn't have to go to school.

But soon we would see the snowplow coming, cutting through the drifts, slicing the snow, chopping it up and blowing it into a huge spewing stream in the ditch. When the plow passed, we were free to go to the store, and I could return to school.

Resentments are like snowdrifts and forgiveness is the snowplow. You see, in the eyes of many people, forgiveness is simply a matter of passive acquittal. But in the Christian context, forgiveness is removing barriers, permitting communication to be restored.

A lot of resentments can build up in our lives in the course of a day. And the only way to put joy on your face and in your heart is to find an overwhelming love that can remove resentments and fill you with forgiveness. "I forgive you" is the language of love!

Today, I am immune to resentments and grudges because I speak the language of love!

Regeneration...The Seed of Success

"The Lord will give you an abundance of good things . . . just as he promised."
                                    Deuteronomy 28:11

In 1977 Anthony Mueller of Pleasant Plains, Ohio, lost over half of his soybean crop. The weather had been bad that year, too wet. Walking through the fields, picking up what he could, he saw a most extraordinary, unusual-looking soybean plant. Shocked by its size and good appearance, he carefully picked off the 202 pods, opened them, collected 503 soybeans, and dried them out. In 1978 he planted 503 soybean seeds in a little plot behind his house; and in October, he harvested 32 pounds! He dried out the seeds, planted them in 1979 on one acre, and harvested 24,019 pounds! In 1980, covering all of his 68 acres, he harvested 2,100 bushels and cashed them out for $15,000.

When you accept Jesus Christ into your life, a seed drops into your soul. And something begins to happen! Remember, "Anyone can count the seeds in an apple. Only God can count all the apples in one seed." We are unable to comprehend the kind of multiplication Jesus uses when He blesses a life that is turned over to Him.

Only God can count the many people who will benefit by my life.

Regeneration...The Seed of Success

"Out of weakness shall come strength!"
Hebrews 11:34

Max Cleland in his book, *Strong at the Broken Places*, states that the place in which a bone breaks and heals will be so strong it will never break there again. In the same way, when the skin is cut and scar tissue forms, the wound will be tougher than the rest of the skin. And when you are tender and soft and exposed to the rough streets of life, you'll develop callouses. You will be strong in the weakest places.

God has given everyone the blessing of a weakness. Weakness is intended to be a blessing! I believe God will let nothing happen to you unless He knows that by His grace and through your faith in Him, you can turn the problem into a partner. The hurt can become your halo. The scar can become a star. Out of your weakness shall come strength—when God is in it.

Be in my weakness, Lord, and make me strong in the broken places.

Regeneration...The Seed of Success

"Each time he said, 'No. But I am with you; that is all you need. My power shows up best in weak people.'"

II Corinthians 12:9

The President of the United States, Ronald Reagan, proclaimed 1981 to be the International Year of the Disabled. He emphasized that the disabled have vast possibilities and potentialities for helping the rest of the human family. And they really do!

Our interest in the handicapped is not new. Actually the ministry of the Crystal Cathedral was the result of one disabled person. When my wife and I came to California to begin a church, all I had was $500 and a dream. We couldn't find a chapel, empty hall or school building to rent for Sunday worship. Finally, in desperation, we used a drive-in theater.

Yet all along I prayed that the months would quickly pass, and we could raise money, find land, build a chapel and worship in a "civilized" Christian way.

Unknown to me, a totally paralyzed woman, Rosie Gray, was in attendance. Her husband responded to our newspaper ad, "Worship as you are, in the family car!" And the old rancher lifted his 72-year-old, paralyzed wife into their car and brought her to that drive-in theater because it was the only church she could attend. God had begun to plant his seeds.

**When a seed is planted,
a life begins to change.**

Regeneration...The Seed of Success

"Give your burdens to the Lord. He will carry them. He will not permit the godly to slip or fall."
Psalm 55:22

Years before, Rosie Gray had suffered a stroke. She could not walk, talk or control her actions. By outward indications, she was totally out of it. The truth was, however, she had a clear mind and understood everything she heard.

We were ready to make the move out of the drive-in and into our new church home, when Warren asked me to call on them. Meeting me at the front door of their ranch, he said, "Before you meet Rosie, I must tell you she had a stroke some years ago. You may think she doesn't understand, but she does! And we'd like to join your church."

As I knelt by her bedside, I asked, "Rosie, do you love Jesus?" Without nodding her head or blinking her eyes, she answered my question as one small tear rolled down her cheek. The following Sunday the Grays were received as charter members of the church. Meanwhile, the congregation prepared to move into the little chapel with new carpeting, upholstered pews, stained-glass windows, and beautiful woodwork.

But I had a nagging problem—what would we do with Rosie Gray? She couldn't sit in a wheelchair. She either had to be strapped to a bed or to the seat of the car. God had begun to grow his seeds.

**The seed of spirituality grows
in the new Christian.**

Regeneration...The Seed of Success

"And let us not get tired of doing what is right, for after a while we will reap a harvest of blessing if we don't get discouraged and give up."
                              Galatians 6:9

Confronted with the reality of the handicapped, we decided to conduct two services each Sunday. At 9:30 we worshipped in our new little chapel, then I dashed out to the nearby drive-in and preached to Rosie, Warren and others who came in their cars.

According to the doctors, Rosie did not have long to live. Yet as the months went by she did not die. Another rainy winter came, and I bought a new umbrella. Summer came and Rosie was doing exceptionally well. For six years I continued to stand under the open sky in the cold or rain, preaching to those who worshipped in their cars.

Then God gave us a new concept! We bought ten acres of land and built a large building with open doors so that I could talk to people seated inside and those outside in their cars at the same time! This church has always realized that although a person may be handicapped, he has great possibilities. If it had not been for Rosie Gray, this ministry would never have become what God intended it to be.

God was harvesting his seeds. And thousands have benefited from the seeds He planted.

I will nourish the seeds you've planted in me, Lord, so my harvest will be abundant!

Regeneration...The Seed of Success

"And some (seed) fell on good soil, and produced a crop that was thirty, sixty, and even a hundred times as much as he had planted."

Matthew 13:8

My philosophy and theology of possibility-thinking was highly shaped by Dr. Victor Frankl when he told me the story of how he, a Jew, was brought before the gestapo in Germany.

They stripped him naked and demanded his wedding band. As he stood there, stark naked, removing his ring—the wedding band that was given to him by his wife who would be exterminated in the ovens—he thought, "There's one thing nobody can take from me—my freedom to choose how I will react to what happens to me."

On the strength of that concept, he not only survived the Holocaust, but he also developed his whole psychiatric system called Logotherapy. Nobody can take from you your freedom to choose what you will do with what happens to you. Life has a way of coloring your personality, but you choose the colors with your own reaction.

When you choose Jesus, He gives you the strength to make other choices in your life. He can multiply the good in your life a hundredfold if you will let Him.

I am excited because God is working in my life.

Regeneration...The Seed of Success

"No matter what happens, always be thankful, for this is God's will for you who belong to Christ Jesus."

1 Thessalonians 5:18

When you face your mountain, your burden, your handicap, you have to know what your options are. It is easy to make a decision when you know all of your options. These are the ways you can handle your hurts:

You can *curse* them.
You can *nurse* them.
You can *rehearse* them.
You can *disperse* them.
Or, you can *reverse* them.

You disperse your hurt when you reverse it. Reversing it means you turn it inside out. Turn your frustration into a fruitful experience.

Where is your weakness? In your business? In your relationships? In your career? Where is the area of your life you need to grow? Intellectually? Spiritually? Physically? Emotionally? What is your biggest fault? Be honest. Remember when you are tackling your biggest burden, out of your weakness shall come strength! God specializes in matching His ability to our disability!

God will match His ability to my disability!

Caring...The Deeds of Success

"Then, when Job prayed for his friends, the Lord restored his wealth and happiness! In fact, the Lord gave him twice as much as before!"

Job 42:10

Some of the richest people in this country never had the goal of acquiring wealth!

Andrew Carnegie's goal was to build a powerful, productive nation, and his theory was to bring the price of steel down from $160 a ton to $20 a ton. He succeeded; and in the process became very wealthy. He was so grateful, he found ways to give away his money. One of these was to establish libraries where all could benefit.

Gillette who wanted every man to be able to afford a clean shave; Ford who felt the joy of owning a car should be shared by everyone; and Ingersoll whose wish was to make a quality inexpensive watch so anyone could own one—all of these men became wealthy because they cared! They cared about others. Their lives showed it! Their deeds proved it!

Caring about others is the road to success!

Caring...The Deeds of Success

"I will instruct you (says the Lord) and guide you along the best pathway for your life; I will advise you and watch your progress."

Psalm 32:8

If you ever experience tension, stress or internal difficulties, the odds are, you have a communication problem. Eventually everything comes down to communication—with your inner self, other persons, and the environment. To really study life, approach it from a communication standpoint: how people communicate with people; and how people communicate with other creatures.

My two youngest daughters gave me a cockatiel for my birthday. It is a beautiful bird. And daily I speak to it in an effort to train it to imitate me. After about two weeks, I walked up to the cage and said, "Hello, Captain!" He looks like a Captain with his crown. He cocked his head, opened his eye, blinked once and stared at me. I said, "God loves you and so do I." Do you know what he did? It's incredible! He looked right at me and said, "Ssss, Ssss!" It almost sounded like yes, yes! God cares for all his creatures, and they seem to know it. But His greatest love is reserved for his children, those who seek Him and ask for His guidance.

I do not always understand what is happening in my life, but I can thank God always for He is with me!

Caring...The Deeds of Success

"Yes, Lord, let your constant love surround us, for our hopes are in you alone."

Psalm 33:22

A maitre d' in a New York City restaurant greeted me, "Dr. Schuller, how are you and Mrs. Schuller?" I replied, "Things have to be good. If they're not getting better, then they're getting worse. That means I've capitulated to a situation that's negative. And I could never do that. One must never capitulate to a situation that is negative." "That's right," he said, "life is too beautiful to give up hope!"

If you're stressful or if you have a problem with yourself or another person, remember that it's a communication problem. Since life is too beautiful to give up hope, you have to care enough to learn to communicate!

Jesus is the source of communication. He showed us that we do not communicate with some obscure indefinite supernatural being, but with someone very real. Jesus came to be our greatest friend, our strongest support, our eternal Savior. Today, you can know Him in a way you have never known Him before. It begins with communication.

Lord, teach me to communicate with my heart more than my tongue!

Caring...The Deeds of Success

"And when he prays to God, God will hear and answer and receive him with joy, and return him to his duties."

Job 33:26

A dear friend of mine is a rabbi. He's a very public person and always has his secretary answer the telephone. He told this story of a time when she was on vacation.

"My secretary, Shirley, was off for the day. The phone rang, and I was going to ignore it. But my love for people overpowered me. So I picked up the phone and said, 'Hello.' The voice said, 'Is Shirley there?' 'No, she's not here this morning,' I replied. 'Will she be there this afternoon?' 'No.' The person went on, 'Tomorrow morning?' 'No,' I said, 'She's off all weekend.' 'Well, what about Saturday?' 'Saturday is the synagogue service.' 'Oh, of course,' the voice replied. 'When can I get in touch with her?' the person persisted. I said, 'Try Monday.' 'What time?' 'Between nine and twelve.' Then the voice said, 'To whom am I speaking?' And I said, 'This is a recording.' and hung up!"

Communication is challenging! You communicate with me, and I with you. But the highest level of communication is when we communicate with a higher presence. We call it prayer, which is simply talking with our dearest Friend, Jesus. It is through our relationship with Him that we learn to really love and care for others. To care enough *is* to learn to communicate.

Jesus is spending the day with me today, and we can talk anytime!

Caring...The Deeds of Success

"Brethren, whatsoever things are true; whatsoever things are honest, whatsoever things are just....think on these things."
                                        Philippians 4:8

Here is an example of a communication problem. In a restaurant, a woman sitting nearby was causing a terrible fuss. She called the waiter over and asked him to turn the air-conditioner down. He agreed and left. Later the woman was fanning herself. She called the waiter back and said, "You know, now it's too warm. You turned the air down too low." The waiter apologized and left again. It wasn't five minutes before the lady was shivering and pulling her coat up around her shoulders. Calling the waiter she said, "It's cold again." The waiter bowed and left. This went back and forth for a while. Finally, we were ready to leave, and the waiter came by our table. I said, "That woman must be driving you crazy." "No," he replied, "We're driving her crazy—we don't have an air-conditioner in this place!"

Communication is so important. How else can we let others know our true feelings? When our communication is dominated by selfishness though, we are doomed to failure. We must care enough to be sure our communication is honest, especially when we communicate with God.

Father, help me to face myself honestly, to communicate openly, and to forgive generously.

Caring...The Deeds of Success

"May God who gives patience, steadiness, and encouragement help you to live in complete harmony with each other—each with the attitude of Christ toward the other."

Romans 15:5

While my son Robert and I were visiting China, he stopped to talk to a group of young boys fishing from a bridge. They responded to him and before long a group of about one hundred young people were gathered. No one interfered.

Two young men emerged from the group, both of them wore thick glasses, looking very bright and intelligent. They were key students at the University of Shanghai. One approached my son pointed to the cross Bob was wearing, and asked, "What's around your neck?" Bob replied, "That's a cross." They continued, "What does it mean?" Bob said, "It means I believe in God." Then Bob presented the four spiritual laws.

1. God loves you even if you don't believe in Him.
2. You, as a human being, are so brilliant that you have the capacity to comprehend the possibility of God.
3. God can forgive your sins.
4. God came to us in human form to show us He exists.

Then Bob led them in a prayer of relinquishment, as one student translated for the rest of the group. The students asked Christ to come into their hearts. With tears in their eyes, they hugged each other. "Brothers," they said as they parted.

God cared enough to give His very best—His son!

Caring...The Deeds of Success

"If you being imperfect know how to give good gifts to your children, how much more shall your father in heaven give good things to those who ask him."

Matthew 7:11

What is the purpose of communication between you and God? What is the purpose of prayer? God wants you to return to Him. He wants you to be in your natural state. He wants you to live as if the earth were a garden—a garden where you can be the kind of person who reflects love. God wants the earth to be a beautiful garden, but no flower, bird, or fern is as beautiful as the face of a human being who smiles with Christ's love.

A city man rode through the country and saw a farmer by his beautiful rows of corn and wheat. The city man said to the farmer, "What a beautiful field God has created." "Yes," the farmer replied, "but you should have seen it when the Lord had it all by Himself."

God needs us. That's what life is all about. You can communicate with God. He knows your needs. In prayer He will meet them. More things are wrought by prayer than this world has ever dreamed of.

Today my smile will contain Christ's love.

Redemption...The Beads of Success

*"For it is from God alone that you have your life
through Christ Jesus. He showed us God's plan
of salvation; he was the one who made us
acceptable to God; he made us pure and holy and
gave himself to purchase our salvation."*
                                I Corinthians 1:30

When you experience salvation, you begin to fully
understand you are somebody! Old or young. Thin or
fat. Rich or poor. You are a precious gem, bought and
paid for by the blood of our Savior.
    "Jesus loves me, this I know.
    For the Bible tells me so."
He loves you and He loves me. I don't believe He's
wrong. I think maybe we just don't understand what
value there is in each of us. We are children of God;
and like the children born in this world, we can take
no credit for that reality. But we can realize that Christ
loves us.
    When you know Christ loves you, you dare to love
yourself. Further you dare to love others, which enables
you to become unselfish. Then you will make the great
discovery that it's possible to live beyond the possibility
of failure. There's no way you can fail if you really
love. When you have the confidence of who you are,
you're free to love. Every person can excel at one
thing—being loving and affirming.

**The cross of Jesus has made me worthy
to stand before God!**

Redemption...The Beads of Success

"We are more than conquerors through Christ who loves us and gave himself for us."
Romans 8:37

Many brides remember three things about their weddings: the aisle they walk down, the altar where they kneel, and the hymn. It's no wonder they may approach marriage with an "I'll alter him," attitude!

Now, that's not only a temptation in marriage, but it's a temptation in all of life. Stop and think of it. In most relationships there is a subconscious, presumptuous, combative attitude: *who's going to win in the relationship game?* It's an attitude that many professors have. They want to conquer their students. It's an attitude that some salesmen have. They want to conquer their challenge and the hard-to-sell fellow.

But there is something better than conquering. The attitude to have in any relationship is not the attitude of winning, but the attitude of redeeming!

During the Civil War, someone told Abraham Lincoln: "You've got an enemy, and somehow you have to get rid of him. Slay him." And Abe Lincoln said, "If I turn my enemy into a friend, have I not slain my enemy?"

**Today, through Christ, I am more
than conqueror!**

Redemption…The Beads of Success

"He died for our sins just as God our Father planned, and rescued us from this evil world in which we live."

Galatians 1:4

My mother was a great person who influenced my life. A successful mother doesn't try to manipulate her child. She doesn't try to intimidate her child so that she can manage him all his life. A successful mother doesn't manipulate or intimidate, she motivates!

Life is more than conquering—it's redeeming. Redemption means to release the positive potential that God put within us until we become the person He wants us to be. We are more than conquerors through Christ who loves us and gave Himself for us. Conquering is not enough!

Thank God the United States realized this after the second World War. We didn't just devastate Japan and Germany, but we became partners with them in rebuilding a new world.

Today you can turn your problem into a partner. That's more than conquering through Christ who loves you.

I am redeemed! The positive potential that God put within me is released!

Redemption...The Beads of Success

"So overflowing is his kindness towards us that he took away all our sins through the blood of his Son, by whom we are saved."
Ephesians 1:7

One of the most inspiring women in our congregation was Sarah Rasmussen. I told her story in my book, *Move Ahead with Possibility Thinking*. Sarah and Norm were about to have their fifth child. Since they already had four sons, they prayed for a girl. At the baby shower, all the gifts were wrapped in pink paper and tied with pink ribbons. Their daughter Leah was born, but a few months later they found out she was Down Syndrome.

They decided not to try to conquer their problem, but to redeem it. They loved little Leah, and as she became a junior high student, she needed peer companionship. So they went to various California adoption agencies and brought mongoloid children that nobody else wanted into their home. Soon they had five of these children join their family.

Finally, they moved up to a big old house with lots of empty land where, the last I heard, Sarah and her husband had about 26 of these children. They turned their problem into a partner. They are more than conquerors through Christ who loves us.

God and I are working to turn my troubles into triumphs!

Redemption...The Beads of Success

"Be full of love for others, following the example of Christ who loved you and gave himself to God as a sacrifice to take away your sins. And God was pleased, for Christ's love for you was like sweet perfume to him."

Ephesians 5:2

You and I have been a problem to God many times. What has He done? He turned His problem into a project. That is the cross of Jesus Christ!

God's problem became Christ's project. Christ came not to destroy or destine us to hell, or simply to save us. He had more in store than just our salvation. He had a plan of partnership in mind. God turned his problem into a partnership so now every Christian is a collaborater with Christ. We are the people that God is pinning all His hopes on.

If you make a commitment of your life to Jesus Christ, you'll stop being God's problem, and you'll start being His partner. That's more than conquering. That's redeeming through Christ Who loves you.

**I am no longer God's problem,
I am His partner!**

POWER TO MAKE YOUR DREAMS COME TRUE

Turn-Around Power

"Sing to Him a new song, play skillfully on the strings, with loud shouts."

Psalm 33:3

The beginning of a new life is to determine that you are going to sing a new song. And that means you have to make a new recording and get rid of some of the old records.

What I'm saying is, we all have a great collection of subconscious tape recordings. And there are a lot of *negative records* in your life and in mine that we have yet to discover and destroy. "O sing to the Lord a new song." Let's make new recordings and that means that we will be on our way!

I'm going to sing a new song.

Turn-Around Power

*"Praise the Lord! Sing to the Lord a new song,
his praise in the assembly of the faithful!"*
                                        Psalm 149:1

I saw an ad the other day in the newspaper advertising a huge piece of earth-moving equipment, and the bold words were TURN-AROUND POWER. Built into that huge machine was turnaround power. For a quarter of a century I have been a pastor and I've counseled with people, young and old, in every conceivable situation, and I have never met a person in whom God did not build turnaround power. You probably haven't discovered it yet. You probably haven't touched the right button yet. But I believe that God will help you to spot this button, push it, and you will have *turnaround power* and *your life will be turned* around! For many of you this will mean you will experience a conversion.

If you have only one life to live, give yourself a chance to live right. Use your God-given built-in turnaround power to destroy some of those old negative excuses and well-worn negative thoughts.

God gives me turn-around power

Turn-Around Power

"O sing to the Lord a new song, for He has done marvelous things!"

Psalm 98:1

There are some old records in your brain that are very dangerous to you. You need to discover them and destroy them. Maybe the record says, "I can't break this habit." Or, "I can't succeed." Or, "I always try and fail." Maybe the record says, "There is no God, not with all this evil in the world." Or, "Christians are all a bunch of hypocrites." All of these are negative, cynical records. I don't know which one is you, but I know one thing: You've got some old records you need to break, too. Reach for a new life. Break the old records. "Sing to the Lord a new song."

**I can break the old records
and reach for a new life**

Turn-Around Power

"Raise yourself, my soul! Arise, O harp and lyre! Let us greet the dawn with a song!"
                                        Psalm 57:8

Run to the light. Those old negatives in your brain are dark corners. They're not illuminating you. They're not inspiring you. They're not enlightening you.

One morning before dawn I went out for a long run. I reached an intersection point where I would have to either keep on going east or turn to the south or the north. If I kept running east, I would follow what was a growing, golden glow; I knew I would catch the daybreak, and I would feel the first long shafts of golden sunlight falling on my chilly cheeks and cold forehead. There had been times when at that same intersection I had turned the other direction. But every time I did I ended up running with my back to the daybreak, and that's disappointing. You feel you are missing out on something beautiful. So I had an easy decision. *I ran to the sunrise!* And I was not disappointed. When I reached the top of the hill the sun hit my face, the bursting light and glory was like being born again.

I will run to the sunrise

Turn-Around Power

"For the commandment is a lamp; and the law is light; and reproofs of instruction are the way of life."

Proverbs 6:23

How do you run to the light? You run to the light of the Word of God.

The Bible is the wisest book ever written. There is unity in truth. A truth is a truth is a truth. You can't say it is a psychological truth and not a biblical truth. If it is a biblical truth and it relates to human nature, it is a psychological truth. And if there is a psychological truth about human nature, you can be positive that it is in the Bible. Perhaps the psychologists just haven't found it yet, but it's there.

We have the answer. We have the key. We have the way. Reach for a new life. This simple and only lesson to you is enough to get you started.

I will run to the light of the Word of God

Turn-Around Power

"The people which sat in darkness saw a great light."

Matthew 4:16

Learn *two words that can put a new song into your life.* The words are *goodbye* and *hello.* Use these words to break the old negative records of cynicism, doubt, anger, hate, suspicion, distrust and unbelief. When these negative emotions come at you and you are tempted to react the way you have reacted for thirty, forty or fifty years, say to yourself, "Here I am doubting again. Here I am putting that beautiful person down again. I haven't grown in many years, unless I've grown more cynical and doubtful." Say goodbye to an old life and say hello to new emotions of faith, belief, hope and love.

Now this may require an act of God, and I indeed think it does. But this is where salvation comes in. The Bible speaks of a person being born again! It really happens. You can become a new creature if you will begin by running to the light. And the light, even the sun, is Jesus Christ. Run to Him!

**I will run to the light of the Son of God—
Jesus Christ**

Turn-Around Power

"Which is as a bridegroom coming out of his chamber, and rejoiceth as a strong man to run a race."

Psalm 19:5

If you have failed in your marriage, your interpersonal relationships, your academic pursuits, in maintaining your own physical or spiritual health, you still can be a winner. If you feel in some way you are or have been a loser, then this message is for you: *Losers can be winners, too!*

I want you to imagine this picture in your mind's eye. I want you to visualize racers running around a track. There is one person leading the race with others following close behind. But there is one person trailing far in the rear. Imagine yourself as the last person in the race with a great space between you and the others who are leading and running to win. Suddenly the announcer says, "The man who is trailing is closing the gap!" The crowd is on its feet. As they draw near to the wire, the man in last place is cutting to the outside. The announcer yells, "It's a photofinish! *You Won!* It's the upset of the day!"

Losers can be winners too

Turn-Around Power

"Weeping may go on all night, but in the morning there is joy."

Psalm 30:5

I know a person who flunked the first and fourth grades and went on to become an astronaut. His name is Ed Gibson.

I'm thinking of someone who ran for office seven times and was defeated every time and still went on to become President. His name was Abraham Lincoln.

I'm thinking of somebody who was kicked out of the psychiatric society, in Vienna, Austria, and went on to become the most prominent, respected psychiatrist in the world today. He is my friend, Dr. Viktor Frankl.

I'm thinking of another person who flunked the first grade and went on to become attorney general. His name was Bobby Kennedy.

I know someone who flunked an English course in college and the teacher said to him, "You might make a living talking but don't try to write books." And he's had ten books published successfully.

I believe losers can become winners.

I can become a big winner

Turn-Around Power

"I can do all things in Him who strengthens me."
Philippians 4:13

If you are trailing at the end of the race, you can pull out of the outside. And when you hit the wire, you can be at the head of the pack. First prizes don't always go to the brightest and strongest person. Again and again the one who wins is the one who is sure that he or she can.

The message here is "hang in there." "When the going gets tough, the tough get going!"

Believe in yourself, and believe in a big God. Believe you can...and you will!

With the help of God, I'm sure I can win

Goal-Reaching Power

"No man, having put his hand to the plough, and looking back, is fit for the kingdom of God."
                                        Luke 9:62

There is a better life for you if you will discover the principles for successful goal setting. Because ultimately *where you are* and *where you will go* depends upon what goals you have set or will set for yourself. Principles of goal setting are what I want to share with you these next several days.

The secret of success is to set the right goals and never take your eye off of them.

Set a goal and keep your eye on it

Goal-Reaching Power

"I have set before you life or death, blessing or curse. Oh, that you would choose life."
                                        Deut. 30:19

You can choose to be a blessing or you can choose to be the kind of person who is a curse to those who have to live with you. "I have set before you life or death, therefore choose life."

The exciting thing about this is that everyone is given the power and the freedom, by God, to choose what kind of a life he wants to live, what he wants to accomplish, and what he wants to achieve. It all begins with goal setting.

I will choose to be a blessing to others

Goal-Reaching Power

"Of this I am convinced, that He who has begun a good work in you will bring it to completion in the day of Christ Jesus."

Philippians 1:6

We conduct Institutes for Successful Church Leadership. Over 4,000 ministers and church leaders from around the world have attended these institutes and a thousand more will attend this year alone.

I received a letter recently from a pastor in Australia. He wrote: "Never before, until I attended the Institute, had I heard of possibility thinking. These concepts have radically changed my ministry. You see, the Bishop told me that his prognosis for my church was gradual decline and closure, with the remnant of the congregation being split between two neighboring churches until they became small enough to close them.

Upon his return to Australia, the first thing he decided to do was set a goal of increasing the Christmas congregation. And in fact, his attendance was twenty-five percent more than last year. He tells how they changed their whole concept of worship and how they changed their whole format. The church is starting to grow and it's going to have great success.

Possibility thinking can radically change my life

Goal-Reaching Power

"And the Lord went before them by day in a pillar of a cloud, to lead them the way; and by night in a pillar of fire, to give them light, to go by day and night."

Exodus 13:21

The mental attitude you have will determine the goals you set. And the goals you set more than anything else will determine where you will end up in life, whether it's a spiritual goal, a personal goal, a professional goal or your family goal. It makes no difference.

Dr. Viktor Frankl from Vienna, Austria, says that goals are great. Indeed, it can be quite disastrous if you set and don't make it and have a negative attitude toward it, *but not reaching your goal isn't as dangerous as not having a goal.* He points to the Old Testament story of how God always kept a pillar of fire in front of the people at night and a cloud by day to pull the people forward. That's what goals do to us. You never catch up with the cloud. You never catch up with the fire. And the *is* must never catch up with the *ought.* If you set a goal and then reach it and can't expand it, you start dying.

The *is* must never catch up with the *ought*

Goal-Reaching Power

"With mankind this is impossible, but with God all things are possible."

Matthew 19:26

When you set your private goals, your personal goals, your spiritual goals or your professional goals, begin with possibility thinking. And what is that? Possibility thinking is the assumption that if it is a beautiful idea, if it is a great thing for God, if it would help people who are suffering, then of course, there must be a way! So goals always rise out of problems—never out of "ego tripping"!

In setting your goals assume that it is possible, even though it may appear impossible.

I can do all things through Christ

Goal-Reaching Power

". . . . Anything is possible if you have faith."
Mark 9:23

Adela Rogers St. John has written a marvelous book entitled, "Some Are Born Great." In it she tells the story of Rachael Carson, who wrote, Silent Spring. In the book there is this dialogue between Alice and the Red Queen. Alice says, "One can't believe impossible things." And the queen says, "I dare say, you haven't had much practice. When I was your age, I always did it for half an hour a day. Why, sometimes I believed in as many as six impossible things before I had breakfast." "And that," says Rachael Carson, "is a very necessary thing to do and to know. If you start believing in impossible things before breakfast, the first thing you know by dinnertime they are not impossible anymore." It begins with possibility thinking.

**By believing in impossible goals,
I make them possible**

Goal-Reaching Power

"Fix your thoughts on what is true and good and right. Think about things that are pure and lovely, and dwell on the fine, good things in others. Think about all you can praise God for and be glad about."

Philippians 4:8

Let your value system guide you. Your goals must be *compatible* or they will be *combatible.* Unless they are compatible with your own deepest value system, they will be combatible. Then you will have tension, guilt and anxiety inside of you and you won't be able to succeed. At your deepest level you must ask yourself, "What did I believe as a child?" "What were the deepest, purest, greatest ideals I ever looked up to?" Perhaps today you're cynical or tarnished. Maybe you've separated yourself from these great moral ideals that you once held. I say to you, in setting your goals go back to your highest values and your highest ideals and make certain that whatever goals you are setting for yourself professionally, spiritually or in any way that they are compatible with these high, God-inspired ideals. If they are not, you won't be able to give it all you've got!

That's why ultimately only the honest man enjoys happy success.

I will let my value system guide me

Goal-Reaching Power

"But the godly shall flourish like palm trees, and grow tall as the cedars of Lebanon."
Psalm 92:12

Aim at growth in quality and quantity. Avoid the cop-out trap of saying, "We're not growing in numbers but we are sure growing in quality." If you really improve in quality, you're going to improve in quantity, unless you've saturated yourself with your product. That means, then, if you aim in your goal setting, you look for growth-restricting areas. What is restricting the growth of our company or *my own personality*? Leadership looks for growth-restricting obstacles and sets goals accordingly. Leadership develops possible ways in which growth-restricting obstacles can be corrected so that the individual or institution can grow as large as it can.

I will aim at growth in quality and quantity

Goal-Reaching Power

"The way of a fool is right in his or her own eyes, but a wise person listens to advice."

Proverbs 12:15

Look and study very carefully your prejudices, your passions and your concerns. Chances are, it will be in these areas that you will discover your blind spots. For your goal-setting should aim at elementary personal blind spots. And we all have them. In other words, if you feel very deeply and passionately on some prejudicial issue, I would advise you to look at it very carefully and just play a game and take the other side of the coin. Try putting yourself in the other guy's shoes. You may be led into an area of your emotional life where growth and maturity are deeply called for.

With God's help, I will put myself in the other person's shoes

Goal-Reaching Power

"Commit your work to the Lord, and your plans will be established."

Proverbs 16:3

Check the success potential before you set your goal. You can almost always check whether an idea will be a failure or a success before you begin by asking, is it practical? Does it fill a vital human need? Can it excel? Can it inspire? Is it pace-setting? Can your idea really meet a need? Can it be inspirational? Can you package it in such a way that people will want it? Will it touch them emotionally? If you're the first with the most, you can't lose unless you don't have the nerve to move ahead.

**I'll be the first with the most—
with the nerve to move ahead**

Goal-Reaching Power

"But I have trusted in your steadfast love; my heart shall rejoice in your salvation."

Psalm 13:5

In setting goals *don't surrender leadership to problems.* Keep a positive attitude toward problems when you set your goals. Never bring the problem-solving phase into the decision-making phase. Don't let your problems take command; let possibilities take command! If you don't make the decision until you solve the problem, by the time you make the decision somebody else will have done it ahead of you. Furthermore, most problem-solving and creative thinking never happens when you're in a phase of indecision. When you make the decision, make the plunge because it's a great idea and it would help God and other people! Then you know you've got to sink or swim. In that kind of a situation, the breakthrough ideas will come.

I will not surrender leadership to problems

Goal-Reaching Power

"A person's wisdom makes a face shine."
                              Ecclesiastes 8:1

In all your goal setting, *let your goals become targets but never let them become ceilings. If your goals are not expandable they will be expendable.*

Let me illustrate. Our first church was built on only two acres of land in another part of Garden Grove. I could see that the church could grow only that large in that location and then it would be non-expandable. We wouldn't be able to park the cars. The time comes when you're choked and you can't grow. And what will happen then? Dynamic, creative staff people will drift away. Dynamic creative people can only work in companies, corporations, institutes and situations where there is constant challenge, and replacing them will be the kind of people who don't want to take chances, who don't want to pay high prices and who do want to take it easy. That will be the new leadership. And even a dead fish can float downstream.

**If the goal is not expandable
it is expendable!**

Goal-Reaching Power

"Let us then approach the throne of grace with assurance, so that we may receive mercy and find grace to help us in time of need."

Hebrews 4:16

Let the size of your God set the size of your dream. Make your goals big enough for God to fit in.

Remember, you can never do anything by yourself. If you are a success it will only be because *others made you successful!* It is your responsibility to set your goals—God will use *others* to make them come to pass! That means you begin by drawing support first of all from God Himself. I don't believe that any person will be a happy success without God.

I want to ask you one question: Are you happy with the goals you've set for yourself? If not, you're free to set new goals. Don't tell me you're too old. Don't tell me you don't have the money. Don't tell me you don't have the connections, the brain power or the will power. That's locked-in thinking. Assuming that there is a solution to every problem, what goals would you set for yourself today?

**Make your goals big enough
for God to fit in**

Problem-Solving Power

"For I am persuaded, that neither death, nor life, nor angels, nor principalities, nor powers, nor things to come, nor height, nor depth, nor any other creature, shall be able to separate us from the love of God, which is in Jesus our Lord."
Romans 8:38-39

I want to talk about problems because you can never reach out without running into them. It's all important that you develop a positive attitude toward problems.

Let me suggest four attitudinal philosophies toward problems. Two are positive and two are negative. You have four choices when you run into any problem. Your first choice is to *resent* it. Your second choice is to simply *consent* to it. Your third choice is to *invent* a solution. And your fourth possibility is to *prevent* the problem from getting worse and from coming back at you later.

I will develop a positive attitude toward problems

Problem-Solving Power

"So we do not lose heart. Though our outer nature is wasting away, our inner nature is being renewed everyday."

II Corinthians 4:16

When a problem hits you, you can simply decide to consent to it—give up and accept defeat. Quit praying, quit practicing possibility thinking and be a total negative thinker. If you do, though, everything will get darker and your road ahead will be paved with catastrophe.

The second option in facing a problem is to resent it. That will make you tough, hard, cold and bitter. You'll feel sorry for yourself. You'll eventually arrive at the end of the road of self-pity—lonely, isolated and unloved.

So, confront your problems—face to face. If you consent to them or resent them, you'll greatly increase your potential for being miserable.

With God's help, I will face my problems

Problem-Solving Power

"And we know that all that happens to us is working for our good if we love God and are fitting into His plans."

Romans 8:28

A good option toward problems is to invent solutions. Make sure Jesus Christ is in your life, so you will have His Holy Spirit to guide you.

Inventing solutions—that's possibility thinking! Once there was a railroad express clerk in Minnesota. One day he received a whole box of watches that were to go to the jeweler in town. The jeweler didn't want them, so the clerk had a problem. The distributor who had sent the watches in the first place said the return postage on them was too expensive; he didn't want them back.

So the railroad clerk turned his problem into an opportunity. He invented a creative solution by putting together a small catalog of watches. He drew pictures of them and sent the catalog to other railroad clerks. They bought all the watches. It was so successful that he ordered more watches and enlarged his catalog. The clerk's name? Sears. His catalog? Sears, Roebuck.

I will turn my problems into opportunities

Problem-Solving Power

"And when you draw close to God, God will draw close to you."

James 4:8

Your fourth option in a problem is to prevent it from ever recurring again. Learn from your mistakes and difficulties. Often we have problems because we have neglected spiritual, moral or physical laws. I want to issue you a warning in love: you must live by God's laws if you want to prevent problems from coming back to you. Then truly, if you are in tune with God through Jesus Christ, you can know that He is your friend.

Decide today that God is real. Draw close to Him. If you want to get a handle on God, get a hand on Jesus. Jesus Christ is real. If you invite Him into your life, He will come—flooding you with His beautiful Spirit, bringing you peace of mind. The presence of God. Salvation.

Get a handle on God—get a hand on Jesus

Achieving Power

"For as in Adam all die, even so in Christ shall all be made alive."

I Corinthians 15:32

Christ gives us *relieving* power. What do I mean? He relieves us from original sin. Original sin means that we are born with a negative spiritual bent and dent. It means we don't have the inherent trust that we should have. Somebody might say, "But look, Dr. Schuller, the little baby trusts his mother naturally." That's not true. Dr. Erickson, the world's foremost child psychiatrist, has taught that a child from birth to twelve months has to learn to trust.

To be conceived and born in sin is to be born with a negative self-image. The opposite of that coin, basically, is to be suspicious and fearful. Adam committed a sin. When he did, he became guilty. When he became guilty, he hid in the bushes, having lost his "trusting nature." Immediately he was infected with a negative self image.

Yes, we are "born in the bushes." We are insecure and detached from God. So we naturally become "sinners," and suffer from guilt. *It is this inherent and acquired guilt that contributes enormously to our tendency towards failure. Accept Christ's relieving power.*

Christ gives me relieving power

Achieving Power

"That you might walk worthy of the Lord pleasing him, being fruitful in every good work, and increasing in the knowledge of God."
                                    Colossians 1:10

Once God has relieved you of your basic distrust, you begin to believe that you are a worthy person and that you deserve to succeed too.

You begin to run into people who believe in you! People aren't going to believe in you if you keep telling them you can't do it. Insecure people attract insecure people. Secure people attract secure people. The first thing that happens is that you're attracted to positive-thinking people. They affirm you! They love you! They see the potential in you and they begin to love you because of it!

I am a worthy person and deserve to succeed

Achieving Power

"For because of our faith, He has brought us into this place of highest privilege where we now stand, and we confidently and joyfully look forward to actually becoming all that God has had in mind for us to be."

Romans 5:2

Michelangelo had a huge chunk of marble that had been cast aside by sculptor after sculptor because it was too long and too narrow. When asked what it was for, he said, "I see David." And he chiselled and carved, and when he finished, there was David, standing tall. He saw David in the marble.

Dr. Viktor Frankl told me recently in my office, "Bob, my definition of love is: *love is wanting to uncover the potential in people.*" That's how God loves you. It's how Jesus loves you. He wants to uncover the possibilities within you.

The person you see in your mind is the person you will be!

Achieving Power

"He who heeds instruction is on the path to life, but he who rejects reproof goes astray."
Proverbs 10:17

Achieving power comes by courage. When you have been relieved of your negative self-image and your guilt, you begin to see possibilities within yourself. You have the courage to admit you need help and take training. You begin to study and to learn.

One of the greatest sopranos of all times was Rise Stevens. She tells the story of how she went out for competition hoping to be chosen as the soprano soloist of the air on a national radio network. She prepared for years, hired a great coach and borrowed thousands of dollars to pay for her lessons.

She made it to the semi-finals, but was finally eliminated. Through her tears, she heard her coach tell her, "Miss Stevens, all I can tell you is: *have the courage to face your faults.* Your next lesson will be at 2 o'clock this afternoon."

For two years, they hammered at her faults—and *that* was the beginning of her greatness.

God give me the courage to face my faults

Achieving Power

"Confess your faults one to another, and pray for one another, that ye may be healed. The effectual fervent prayer of a righteous man availeth much."
James 5:16

Jesus gives me the courage to face my faults. I'm not perfect! And I'm not sinless! And I'm making mistakes every day! So are you. But when we are liberated enough to tell the world that we do have sins and faults and we are going to work on them with the help of God, *and that's what gives us achievement power!* Success is never certain: Failure is never final. There is never anybody who will win unless he looks at himself so constructively, positively and self-critically for improvement until he makes it.

"I can do all things in Him who strengthens me." He gives me *relieving* power, *believing* power, and then *achieving* power.

Take Jesus Christ into your life and it will work for you, too.

Jesus Christ gives me the courage to face my faults. I'm not perfect! And I'm not sinless! And I'm making mistakes every day!

Success is never certain—
failure is never final

TUNE INTO YOUR
INNER POSSIBILITIES

Possibilities—They Are Within You!

"Worship and serve God with a clean heart and a willing mind, for the Lord sees every heart and understands and knows every thought. If you seek Him, you will find Him."

I Chronicles 28:9

Find God within you, and begin to succeed in your search for your inner possibilities.

There is no doubt that God made you and me and every creature with enormous latent potential that, beyond question, is not fully discovered by any human being in his lifetime.

There lie in your mind and in mine, seeds, waiting to feel the spring rain of God's creative spirit, when they will sprout, grow and bloom into ideas. *The most powerful force in the world is a positive idea in the mind of a believer who is walking in the will of God.*

I can walk in God's will and He will give me positive ideas

Possibilities—They Are Within You!

"I say to the Lord, 'You are my Lord; I have no good apart from you.'"

Psalm 16:2

One day I was in a board meeting all afternoon. I had gathered with me a great selection of creative minds. We had to come up with creative ideas. But after five continuous hours, none of us had been able to come up with a single good idea.

That evening I drove up into the mountains to the Campus Crusade Headquarters in Arrowhead Springs to lecture. I parked my car there and walked down the lonely trail behind the building where I was to speak.

Suddenly my discouraged mind was over-whelmed and I spoke outloud: "Oh God, I am totally, completely, utterly dependent upon you for any level of achievement or success; because, God, all success depends upon the right idea. And I am utterly, totally dependent upon you for ideas."

As I was driving home after my lecture, I had so many beautiful, great, wonderful, exciting, creative ideas, I had to stop the car to write them down! I shared them with the board, and all of us unanimously agreed they were fantastic ideas. Where did they come from? *God!*

God will give me beautiful, creative ideas

Possibilities—They Are Within You!

"Commit your work to the Lord, and your plans will be established."

Proverbs 16:3

Jim Poppen was a very unpretentious student. He didn't give much promise of being outstanding in success. He thought he would like to be a doctor, but everybody knew he didn't have the grades and the ability for that. But he insisted. So he tried it out at Northwestern University in Chicago, and to everybody's astonishment he graduated. Some years ago as I was on my way from my home to my office, I put the car radio on and heard the first reports of the shooting of Robert Kennedy, who was still alive. The newscaster said that the leading brain surgeon in America was being flown from Boston, Massachusetts, to California. He was Dr. James Poppen.

Inner potential. Inner possibilities. *Only God knows what they are! Don't let people say it can't be done!*

The greatest force in the world is a positive idea in the mind of a believer who is walking in the will of God!

Possibilities—They Are Within You!

"And He said unto me, 'My grace is sufficient for you; for my strength is made perfect in weakness.'"
ness.'"

II Corinthians 12:9

The Washington Bridge has been around since 1883. It was a God-inspired idea. There was an engineer back in the last century named John Roebling, who got the idea: Bridge the river and tie Manhattan Island to the mainland. But all the bridge-building experts in the world told him it could not be done.

John Roebling convinced his son Washington that the bridge could be built, and they developed the concepts of how it could be accomplished, how the obstacles could be overcome. But there was a tragic accident just at the outset. John Roebling was killed; Washington survived but was left with permanent brain damage, unable to walk or talk. And he alone knew how the bridge could be built.

Everybody said to forget it. But Washington developed a code of communication. All he could move was one finger, and he touched the arm of his wife with that finger. He communicated to her what to tell the engineers and how to solve the problems.

That's how Washington Roebling supervised the construction of the Washington Bridge for thirteen years!

You have no idea what you can do when you walk in the center of God's will

Possibilities—They Are Within You!

"Believe in the Lord your God, and you shall have success! Believe His prophets, and everything will be all right!"

II Chronicles 20:20

Romana Banuelos was just 16 years old, living in Mexico, when her husband left her with two little children, poverty stricken. So she and her two babies got on a bus and came to Los Angeles to work, not able to speak a word of English.

She had seven dollars in her pocket. She went to a cab driver and gave him the name and address of a distant relative who lived here in Los Angeles. He delivered her at the house and charged her seven dollars. That was all of her money.

She got a job washing dishes. Then she got a job making tacos from midnight to six in the morning. Then she saved some money and invested $500 in a taco machine. Today she manages the largest Mexican wholesale food business in the world. And she was hand-picked by the President of the United States to be the 37th Treasurer of the United States. Romana has said, "Believe, believe."

Believe, believe! God has given you inner possibilities

Possibilities—They Are Within You!

". . . For the Kingdom of God is within you."
Luke 17:21

Don't put yourself down. Start putting yourself up. God wants you to be successful. What does it mean? Recognize that God has a will for your life and get into the center of that will. How do you do that? You do that by beginning and saying, "God, I have not been living according to your will. I have been doing what I want to do. I have been sinning. I have been disobedient."

I ask you now to think of one area of your life that needs to be cleansed, and cleanse it. Let Jesus Christ come in until you feel you have been born again and you feel the sunshine and you know you are walking in the will of God. Because *the most powerful force in the world is a positive idea in the mind of a believer who is walking in the will of God!*

I decide today to walk in God's will

Nothing Is Impossible

"But you are a chosen race, a royal priesthood, a holy nation, God's own people, that you may declare the wonderful deeds of Him who called you out of darkness into His marvelous light."
                                          I Peter 2:9

I was recently in Shanghai, the heart of modern Communism in China. I walked past the consulate where our government had erected a large glass-covered poster on the wall that encircles the consulate offices. There were pictures and scenes of the United States which the consulate felt would make a great impression upon the millions of modern Chinese who walk down the street. Included was the largest picture of yours truly standing in the Crystal Cathedral. Underneath was written, "Americans are happy people—they believe in God. Faith is very much alive. In fact, not long ago, one of the most beautiful churches built in America was erected and made out of ten thousand six hundred and sixty-eight window panes".

The Crystal Cathedral was used by the federal government of the United States to hopefully make a positive statement of faith to China.

**My life can make a positive statement
of faith to my world**

Nothing Is Impossible

"And the angel said unto them, 'Fear not: for, behold, I bring you good tidings of great joy, which shall be to all people."

Luke 2:10

Gerald Jampolsky once said that the two basic emotions are not love and hate, but love and fear. When you meet somebody whom you think is angry, remember he's not angry. He feels threatened. (Maybe by you.) Fear is the defense mechanism that causes people to feel angry. So, the answer to fear is faith.

Jesus is the answer. He said it all in one single sublime sentence that I summarize this morning. I've thought about it, prayed about it, tried to live by it, and tried to apply it. I've tried to practice it, build my books around it and after 30 years I repeat with greater force this sentence: "If you have faith as a grain of mustard seed you can say to your mountain, 'Move.' And it will move." That is one of the greatest statements ever made by a human being on planet earth, for Jesus is not only God. He was man.

The answer to my fears is faith in God

Nothing Is Impossible

"Where is your father?' they asked. Jesus answered, "You don't know who I am, you don't know who my father is. If you knew me, then you would know Him too."

John 8:19

The first result of sin in the human race was that the first human creature felt worthless, helpless, and hopeless. So God decided to do something about it. He sent his own son, Jesus Christ into the world. God was morally obligated to reveal Himself. Jesus was not just a nice guy. Jesus was and is God coming to earth, making a statement to you and to me. God had to do that. If God had not done so, every religion on planet earth would have its own shot at guessing what God is really like. We wouldn't know what religion to believe in. He had to tell us the truth so that religions would not sprout up and form new cults and with new prophets and new messiahs, who claim to have brilliant insight into what God is really like. Through Jesus, God came to the world to tell us what He was like.

**Through Jesus, I can know God
in a personal way**

Nothing Is Impossible

"For if you had faith even as small as a tiny mustard seed, you could say to this mountain, 'Move!' and it would go far away. Nothing would be impossible."

Matthew 17:20

Miracles happen. Only the other day I encountered a young man who had a huge tumor around his heart. A lot of prayer was determining whether he should undergo surgery or not. The odds of survival were not good. Finally, they made the decision, risky though it was, to go through with it. When they opened his chest, they had the shock of their life. The tumor was gone. It had totally disappeared. They know it was a water cyst that broke. They did not have to touch the heart. They simply sewed him up and today he is fine.

If you have faith—you can say to your mountain, "Move". You have to begin with the assumption that if God wants to, He can perform a miracle. Don't close the door to God, but continue to leave that divine option open for Him, if that is His choice.

With faith—I can move my mountain— miracles happen

Nothing Is Impossible

"Here on earth you will have many trials and sorrows, but cheer up, for I have overcome the world."

John 16:33

A short time ago I preached in a church in Michigan. A dear friend of mine was seated in the front row, smiling enthusiastically. She was a radiant lady, despite the fact that both her legs were artificial.

She was so beautiful. If you have faith as a grain of mustard seed, does it mean that legs will grow back? How does the mountain move? Here is how: If you have a positive faith toward your condition, your perception of the problem will change. When your perception of a problem changes, the problem changes. No longer is it a draining, destructive, defeat-producing experience. Instead, it becomes a challenge, a motivation-force to climb and conquer. When that happens, your mountain has become a miracle! It has moved because of your faith and your attitude. That's what Jesus means.

With Jesus, my problem can become a challenge—my mountain a miracle!

Nothing Is Impossible

"Be glad for all God is planning for you. Be patient in trouble, and prayerful always."
Romans 12:12

If you've got a mountain, pray that it will go away. Then add this phrase: "Lord, if you leave it, help me to welcome it, because it must be a blessing." I prayed for many years that we would never have to build a larger church. The Crystal Cathedral took about 12 years to build: 7 years for us to get into it, then 5 years to develop it. If problems don't go away, turn them into possibilities. That is what faith does.

Faith will turn my problems into possibilities

Nothing Is Impossible

"But thanks be to God, who gives us the victory through our Lord Jesus Christ."
                              I Corinthians 15:57

Marguerite Piazza was a Metropolitan Opera star when her husband died, leaving her alone with six children. At almost the same time, a spot on her cheek was diagnosed as melanoma, a deadly type of cancer.

The beautiful Marguerite was told surgery was her only hope for survival. Doctors would remove her cheek, leaving her face disfigured. The night she received the news, the house had been packed to hear her sing and watch her dance. She recalls, "What do you do at a time like that? You do what you are paid to do. I was paid to lift people. So I prayed. Then I hung my troubles on a hanger and left them in the closet and went onstage and sang my heart out. And danced for all I was worth and the people loved it."

What a victory! Today she is alive and well. She had the cheek removed and she is still beautiful.

Do you have a mountain? Have faith. It will either go away, or you'll see it as a special blessing from God that comes floating to you down the river of tears. *Welcome it!*

I too can have the victory!

Problems? Obstacles? Nevertheless—It's Possible!

*"For the moment all discipline seems painful rather than pleasant, **nevertheless** later it yields the peaceful fruit of righteousness . . ."*
                                        Hebrews 12:11

There is a particular billboard by the freeway that has long inspired me. Every time I see it I get a lift. It's an advertisement for one of the major entertainment parks in Southern California. Plunging out from the center of the billboard is a huge, black reproduction of a whale, and the words, "See Orky the Whale—the World's Biggest Entertainer!" Every time I see Orky leaping through the billboard, I realize I can leap over my problems, too.

But there are times when the zest goes out of life, and you find yourself totally deflated. You not only can't leap over your problems and obstacles, but the zip for life is gone. When the zest goes out of the nest, that is the true test. What do you do?

Life loses its lift not because of the bad that happens to you, and not because of the good that doesn't happen to you, but because of how you perceive and judge what is happening to you!

Given that basis, I have a solution that will help you when you feel you're losing your zest. *When the wind is oozing out of your spirit, and you feel as though you're deflated, then roll out this thundering, conquering, life-inflating word . . . NEVERTHELESS!*

I can leap over my problems too!

Problems? Obstacles? Nevertheless—It's Possible!

*"I suffer many things. **Nevertheless**, I am not ashamed, for I am not defeated . . ."*
                                        II Timothy 1:12

Nevertheless—the big "N"! St. Paul knew that positive thinking was not a Pollyanna faith! So, you got fired last week? Nevertheless, thank God you had a job as long as you did! So, somebody let you down? Nevertheless, there are still many people you can trust. So, your dream turned to ashes? Nevertheless, God still has a future for you if you believe!

When troubles, difficulties, diseases, death, divorce and the negative forces of life surround you like an impenetrable fortress, remember this single, powerful, heavy duty, fantastic word—Nevertheless!

**God has a future for me—
I can turst Him**

Problems? Obstacles? Nevertheless—It's Possible!

*"What turmoil has filled my life. I sometimes see myself as stupid and ignorant. I must seem like an animal to you, O God. **Nevertheless**, You love me. You hold my hand. You keep guiding all my life with Your wisdom and counsel and afterwards You receive me into the halls of Heaven."*

Psalm 73:23

When my daughter, Carol, suffered through the surgeries and pain relative to the amputation of her leg, John Wayne sent her an autographed photo of himself. Written across the bottom of the picture was this simple but profound statement: "Carol, be happy. You're loved!"

Now some people might say, "What a dumb thing to say to a girl who just lost a leg in an accident!" But John Wayne knew better. He was a smart, perceptive guy, and it was reflected in those words. "Be happy—You're loved!" If you're loved you can be happy no matter what happens to you!

Be happy—you're loved!

Problems? Obstacles? Nevertheless—It's Possible!

"Behold, we count them happy which endure. You have heard of the patience of Job, and have seen the end of the Lord; that the Lord is very pitiful, and of tender mercy."

James 5:11

No matter how much your heart is breaking, you can still be happy! Nevertheless holds the key to your happiness!

So your life is filled with pain, *nevertheless*, you are loved!

So you lost a big race, *nevertheless*, you were healthy enough to run!

So you didn't get the credit, *nevertheless*, you did it and you know it!

Nevertheless—that's heavy artillery. It used to be that up until 1916, the only way to fight was by trench warfare. But then the artillery tank was invented and a new battle was fought. The tank rolled over the trenches and across the hills and rivers. It trampled everything under its big, wide, flattening treads.

In the same way, when you fight negative emotions of jealousy, hate, despair, loneliness, defeat, disappointment, you need to roll out the heavy artillery. You need the heavy tank with the big NEVERTHELESS painted across it broadside!

Even if my heart is breaking, I can still be happy!

Problems? Obstacles? Nevertheless—It's Possible!

*"**Nevertheless**, I live by His promise. I look for a new Heaven."*

II Peter 3:13

If you look in the mirror and don't like what you see, remember this word: *Nevertheless! Nevertheless, you can radiate love and joy!*

Maybe you're facing terminal cancer today. Maybe you know you have only two months to live. Maybe you are alone without the companion of your life.

Remember the heavy artillery. Nevertheless! Nevertheless, you are loved! Nevertheless, you have our Lord beside you!

**God is beside me—
I can radiate love and joy!**

Dreaming Makes It Possible

"He died for all so that all who live—having received eternal life from Him—might live no longer for themselves, to please themselves, but to spend their lives pleasing Christ who died and rose again for them."

II Corinthians 5:15

You may say, "Oh, what a wonderful plan God had for your life, Dr. Schuller." The good news I have is that God has the same plan for you. There is no difference between your life and mine. If you think there is, you are wrong. For the truth is, every life is the plan of God, and every plan is the same. God's plan is that we should become the incarnation, the manifestation, the living expression of the reality of the living Christ in the world today. God commissions you to serve and he commissions me to serve when we hear the call to accept Christ into our lives.

God has a wonderful plan for my life

Dreaming Makes It Possible

"But other fell into good ground, and brought forth fruit, some an hundredfold, some sixtyfold, some thirtyfold."

Matthew 13:8

Have you ever thought, "Maybe I'm just a biological accident." Have you ever wondered, "Is there meaning to my existence on Planet Earth?" Have you ever asked the question, "What's the purpose of my life, anyway?" If your life doesn't have real power, purpose, existence and meaning, then this message is for you!

"You have not chosen me, I have chosen you, to bear fruit." What is the mission that I have? What is the mission you have? It is the message that God is alive, that He loves us and that because of His love, we have something to do. Each of us has a calling to share that love, honestly and openly.

God is alive! God loves me!

Dreaming Makes It Possible

"For God so loved the world so much that He gave His only son, so that anyone who believes in Him shall not perish but have eternal life."
John 3:16

Do you know what our message, our mission really is? It is that you are somebody. You bet you are! *You are somebody.* People may not know your name. You may never have fame or wealth. But you are somebody, because Jesus died for you, and God loves you and so do I. There is no message we need to hear in the world today more than this message.

George Gallup and I have been working on a poll of self-esteem in American society. The poll clearly shows that church attendance in America today does not build up one's self-esteem. A personal relationship with God and Jesus Christ *does*, but just attending a ritualistic church does not build self-esteem.

The poll also substantiates what we have long suspected; that a church isn't a true church and the gospel isn't the true Gospel unless it builds people up. God came to earth in Christ to tell you and every human being: *You are somebody!*

I am somebody!

Dreaming Makes It Possible

". . . . for He hath said, 'I will never leave thee nor forsake thee.'"

Hebrews 13:5

You are never alone in life, unless you choose to be. God is always closer to you than you know. He is as close as an idea that penetrates the mind, as close as a mood that can sweep over your spirit, as close as you want Him to be. The beautiful message of the Gospel of Christ is that Christ came into this world, died, and rose to live in your heart.

I once had the memorial service for a beautiful young wife. She was only 31 years old when she had her mastectomy. It was all metastasized, and the cancer had already spread throughout her body. Although she underwent heavy chemotherapy for two years, she knew her end was near. She wrote a letter to her husband. She said, "Honey, when I'm gone, just tuck me in a little corner of your heart, and move on." You are somebody! You're never alone! You have value!

Remember: God is always closer to you than you know.

I never have to be alone

Dreaming Makes It Possible

"And if, as my representatives, you give even a cup of cold water to a little child, you will surely be rewarded."
                              Matthew 10:42

Anyone who does what he or she can for God has infinite value; the nurse in a hospital room, the young man who pumps gas and washes the windshield of the car and touches your life for a moment, the clerk in the store, the custodian who keeps it clean. They are all somebody. Each of their lives has value. Whoever you are, *your* life can touch another life, and *you* can be Christ in action wherever you are.

**My life has value—
I can be Christ in action**

Dreaming Makes It Possible

"For I can do everything God asks me to with the help of Christ who gives me the strength and power."

Philippians 4:13

Janice Terry is only 32 years old, but her heart is so degenerated that she has a very short time to live. Her only possibility for survival is a heart transplant, but she must wait for a donor.

One week she was at a low point, so I tried to comfort her. I prayed with her, and I said, "Janice, you know, you cannot live until someone else dies." She said, "Yes, that is really something." She never knows when, or if, someone will die before she does. I don't think anyone is in a more delicate, sensitive experience right now than this woman whose only hope of living is if somebody dies and donates their heart to her.

As I visited with this brave, young woman, I kept remembering, "I can do all things through Christ who strengthens me." If you are facing a loss, a grief, a hurdle, a mountain, an unsolvable problem, I want to say to you, *"You can succeed. You are somebody. You never need to be alone. Your life has great value. You can overcome."*

I can be an overcomer

Dreaming Makes It Possible

"A perverse man will be filled with the fruit of his ways, and a good man with the fruit of his deeds."
Proverbs 14:14

You have the freedom to choose. Each of you will choose how valuable or how cheap your life is. You alone decide how significant or insignificant your contribution will be.

It all depends, you know, on whom you attach yourself to. *You will become as big as the person you attach yourself to.* That is a principle. Likewise, you become as big as the dream you commit yourself to.

There are no great people in this world. There are only ordinary people. Some people commit themselves to extraordinary goals. Some people dream big dreams and the big dreams make them bigger. Some people make a commitment to a cause and the size of the cause will determine the size of their value. You have the freedom to choose.

**I can choose the value of my life—
I will make it significant!**

Dreaming Makes It Possible

"In all toil there is profit, but mere talk tends only to want."

Proverbs 14:23

There are only two kinds of people on earth today
Two kinds of people, no more I say.
Not the rich and the poor, for to know a man's wealth
You must first know the state of his conscience and health,
Not the happy and sad, for in life's passing years,
Each has his laughter and each has his tears.
No, the two kinds of people on earth I mean
are the people who lift and the people who lean.
In which class are you? Are you lifting the load
of some overtaxed lifter who's going down the road,
Or are you a leaner who lets others share
your portion of toil and labor and care?

Ella Wheeler Wilcox

I will lift the load of another today

Dreaming Makes It Possible

"If then you have been raised with Christ, seek the things that are above, where Christ is, seated at the right hand of God."

Colossians 3:1

You can become tremendously important if you will only attach yourself to somebody who's superimportant. I have that person for you: His name is Jesus Christ! If you've never done it before, accept Him into your life. Then, you'll be born again and He'll be tucked away in a corner of your heart.

I suppose my ministry started 50 years ago when my Uncle Henry said, "You're going to be a minister when you grow up," and I believed it! My life has had value for one simple reason: I attached myself to somebody a lot bigger than I, and His name is Jesus Christ.

Is your life attached to Jesus today? He's there, by your side. Reach out to him now.

**I will permanently attach myself
to Jesus Christ**

It's Possible to Keep Your Dream Alive

"I am the vine, you are the branches. Anyone who abides in me, and I in he or she, you will bear much fruit, for apart from me you can do nothing."
                                                    John 15:5

Are you supportive of Christ and His work today? Some of you are not Christians. You don't claim to be, but God calls you just like he called me 50 years ago, and He says, "I want to live in the corner of your heart." Jesus Christ wants to live in your whole life. To you who are Christians, God wants you to be everything you can be. I invite you today, to stand up and be counted as a friend of Jesus Christ. Share His love as He leads you to share it, day to day, week to week. Make the world a more beautiful place for God.

God commissions you to be a part of the vine, a part of the branch, to graft yourself into Jesus Christ. He is the vine, you are the branch. All of us are commissioned to serve Him, to keep the Good News of the Gospel of Christ spreading far and wide until His Kingdom comes on earth as it is in Heaven.

**I will make the world a
more beautiful place for God**

It's Possible to Keep Your Dream Alive

"And Abram gave him a tenth of everything."
Genesis 14:20

A family made a commitment to our church to tithe. They went home. They looked at the money. They couldn't stretch it. "Unless," he said, "We cut something out." His wife and his friend had been telling him, "You're drinking too much." When someone once hinted that he was an alcoholic, he got angry. He said, "I'm not an alcoholic, I only drink beer."

Every person who belongs to Alcoholics Anonymous knows that most alcoholics only drink beer. But he made a commitment to tithe. A few days later, he went to the liquor store, bought a six-pack and took it home. But instead of drinking it like he usually did, he only looked at it and said, "I just used God's money." He never opened a can. He went to Alcoholics Anonymous. That was 14 years ago! Today he is sober. His marriage is strong.

What new doors will God open in the life of a person who decides to "give something back" from the abundance of God's blessing?

**God will give me the power
to keep my commitments**

It's Possible to Keep Your Dream Alive

"Clap your hands, all peoples! Shout to God with loud songs of joy!"

Psalm 47:1

I know a young lady named Kathy. She's in Seattle undergoing a bone marrow transplant, because it's the only thing that can save her life.

I spoke with her recently on the phone. What powerful faith! She said, "Oh, it's wonderful just to look outdoors and see the sun shining." Kathy is a young mother, not even 30. But she is so grateful just to be alive. Alive. If you are given the gift of life, my friend, and the gift of health, and if you're not living under a death sentence right now, you should be so grateful to God.

List below at least three areas of your life that you can be grateful for today:

1._____

2._____

3._____

I am grateful to God for all my blessings

It's Possible to Keep Your Dream Alive

"Great is the Lord, and greatly to be praised, and His greatness is unsearchable."
                                                    Psalm 145:3

Three years ago, Mrs. Schuller had cancer removed with a mastectomy. Eight days ago, they found another growth and removed it. While we waited to hear the results of the biopsy, I can assure you that we re-evaluated everything. Property didn't mean anything; clothes didn't mean anything; money didn't mean anything. The only thing that mattered was life and living it the way God wants us to.

The next morning the doctor called and said, "Good news—it's benign!" I am so grateful.

"I've often found that God leads us through the valleys so that we can rejoice in the sunrise when we reach the mountain top.

Live your life for God, and trust his loving, guiding hand.

Nothing is as important as living my life for God

GET SET FOR
A MIRACLE

Believe in Miracles

"So God created great sea creatures, and every sort of fish and every kind of bird. And God looked at them with pleasure, and blessed them all."
Genesis 1:21

I love the great California grey whale, massive, beautiful beasts of the deep. Every winter these whales come from their home in the Alaskan waters and migrate to Mexico until they reach a point where the temperature of the water approximates the temperature of the womb of the female cow. At that point she gives birth to her calf. Since the temperature of the water is close to the temperature of the womb, the calf is able to survive the birth, move out of the Mexican waters, heading back up the coast until they arrive once more at their home, which is in the cold waters of Alaska. By the time they've reached that point, the calf's body is adjusted to the change of temperature of the water.

What readjustments is God waiting to do in your life?

Trust him, give yourself over to him, now.

His promise is good—to always be by your side.

God's miracles are all around me

Believe in Miracles

"God has always shown us that these messages are true by signs and wonders and various miracles and giving certain special abilities from the Holy Spirit to those who believe; yes, God has assigned such gifts to each of us."

Hebrews 2:4

How do you spot a whale? Believe it's out there! *Believe* that there is life lurking and moving there beneath the surface that you may not see. When you don't spot it, continue to believe!

Don't look for something dramatic. Look for something quite natural, like an exceptional swirl on the surface of the water. Then watch for a puff of fog. Keep watching, and eventually you'll see a hump of black and maybe even a whole tail, waving in the sun, before it plummets down and disappears.

Look for miracles the way you look for whales. Don't expect something big and dramatic and unnatural. Expect something quite natural, yet with a wonderful, mysterious circumstance. Eventually you will see, with the passing of time, that seemingly trivial event will turn out to be a pivotal turning point in your life! Your whole destiny, it turns out, hinged upon that event over which you had no control whatsoever! Looking back you can only say, "It was an act of God. It was a miracle!"

I believe in miracles!

Believe in Miracles

"How precious is your lovingkindness, O God, so the children of mankind take refuge in the shadow of your wing!"

Psalm 36:7

"Anne and Benno Fischer believe in miracles. They were each the only one of their large families to survive the Jewish extermination of Nazi Germany. Prior to the war and the German takeover of their native Poland, they had been engaged to be married. They had been thrown in separate concentration camps, and each thought the other dead at the end of the war.

Benno went to Stuttgart, Germany with a friend—the one and only time he has ever been in that country—and was waiting on a street corner for a bus. He was surprised to see a girl who looked just like Anne. He couldn't believe it! The girl, suspecting she was being eyed by a stranger, turned around. Shock became pure delight as they fell into each other's arms.

What brought them together? It was a miracle! Many of us have had meetings over which none of us had control. Not manipulated by men, God brought Anne and Benno together.

**God is my miracle worker—
praise His name!**

Expect A Miracle

"Jesus replied, 'The Scriptures also say, Do not put the Lord your God to a foolish test.'"
Luke 4:12

God is not a big boss who throws His power around. To understand God's miracles you have to understand that God has limited His own power. Listen carefully: God's power is restrained. First, by the nature of nature; second, by the nature of man; and third, by the nature of God Himself.

When God built this world, He built into the universe natural laws, like the laws of gravity. God has limited His power with these laws. So God's power is limited, but this is no indignity to His character: God's decision to restrain His power only glorifies Him more.

It is because God is holy that He restrains His power. Unrestrained power means there are no ethics, and you bulldoze, you push your way. No person will ever be able to jump off a building and on the way down say, "God, I'm going to test your power. Please let me fall and not get hurt." Nature doesn't work that way.

Power restrained is power improved

Expect A Miracle

"For this freedom Christ has liberated us."
                                        Galatians 5:1

God made you and He made me with a certain degree of free will. He wants persons, not puppets! He could have created you and me and every human being so that we would be nothing more than brilliant computers responding to a God who sits in heaven at the master control, pushes these buttons, and everything would go along beautifully. There would be no sin. There would be no injustice. There would be no Nazi holocaust. There would be none of this. The only thing is, there would be no persons, only computers. No free will.

God respects the dignity of persons in such a way that He will not overpower your will against your own decision to act.

God respects my dignity—I am free

Expect A Miracle

"Butter and honey shall he eat, that he may know to refuse evil, and choose the good."

Isaiah 7:15

If you decide that you want something and you do not care about the Ten Commandments or the word of God or the teachings of Jesus—God will let you have your way. He respects your independence. He will advise you, but it is ultimately your decision! If you choose not to trust God, of course His miracle power is reduced.

So, as we look at miracles, let's keep this in mind: What is a miracle? A miracle is a beautiful act of God's Providence moving into life, and there are many of them every day.

God's providence moves beautifully in my life every day

Expect A Miracle

"For God says, 'Your cry came to me at a favorable time, when the doors of welcome were wide open. I helped you on a day when salvation was being offered.' Right now God is ready to welcome you. Today He is ready to save you."
                    II Corinthians 6:2

There isn't a week that I don't get letters from people all over the United States saying to me, "Dr. Schuller, I just happened to turn on the television because I wanted to look at maybe a football game or maybe a movie that was coming on. I was turning the dial and suddenly stopped for a moment on your program. And I started listening. I don't go to church. I don't claim to be a believer. The miracle is, I listened to what was being said. Dr. Schuller, I tuned in the following week and then the next week. Today, I know God, I met Him; He's real."

The world calls it chance. Positive thinking people call it, not chance, but *God!*

I know God—He is real

Expect A Miracle

"Surely goodness and mercy shall follow me all the days of my life."

Psalm 23:6

Every single day of my life God's goodness and mercy is going to be shown to me. That means that there is not a single day in your human, earthly existence where God does not do *something* beautiful for you. Now you may not see it, you may not know it, you may not even recognize that this is an act of God within you, but that does not invalidate His activity.

God shows His goodness and mercy to me in beautiful ways

Expect A Miracle

"Come, see the glorious things God has done. What marvelous miracles happen to His people."
                                        Psalm 66:5

I watched a television program where they were discussing the photography of Weston, now deceased, who was one of the greatest photographers of our time. In the backdrop of the conversation, they had one of his famous photographs. It's a beautiful sculptured mountain; in the foreground are three unadorned telephone poles. A novice would look at it and say it's a picture of three telephone poles in front of a hill. The truth is that it is a most unique, creative, composition. As the panel was discussing the picture, the television interviewer said, "Couldn't anybody take a camera, go out there and take the same picture?" One of the critics said, "No! No! Nobody else could do it." "Why not?" asked the interviewer. And the critic replied, "Nobody else would see it."

Miracles are like that. We need to have our spirit attuned to God to be able to see them.

A hundred million miracles are happening every day; but only those who have the faith will spot them on life's way.

Expect A Miracle

"Then Elisha prayed, 'Lord, open his eyes and let him see!' And the Lord opened the young man's eyes so that he could see horses of fire and chariots of fire everywhere upon the mountains."
II Kings 6:17

Why don't we see these miracles that are happening all the time? I think I can answer that question this way: Have you ever been hospitalized, maybe for a few days or a week or more, and then when you recovered enough the hour came when you could go home? When you came out of the hospital, suddenly the whole world looked different—cars, people, sky, trees. You noticed flowers blooming that were blooming when you went in, but you never noticed them. Everything looked different. You had a tremendous, almost ethereal dimension of awareness.

After you came out of the hospital, you saw like you did not see before. There was, for want of a better word, heightened sensitivity in the area of human perception.

Prayer is one way to raise your level of perception.

Decide today to be sensitive to the still quiet voice of God.

God—please give me heightened sensitivity and perception

Count Your Miracles Every Day

"The eye is the lamp of the body. So, if your eye is sound, your whole body will be full of light; but if your eye is not sound, your whole body will be full of darkness. If then the light in you is darkness, how great is the darkness!"

Matthew 6:22-23

A blanket of daily, accumulated anxieties, fears, depressions, jealousies, problems and difficulties keep us from seeing miracles. What blinds us to the tree, the flower, the clouds, the sky, the sparkle in the eye of someone we're talking to? What blinds us to the miracles that God is performing? It is our negative emotional attitude, or our fears and our worries and our concerns and our anxieties. It's the bad news we've just heard or the bad news we are expecting when we go to the mailbox and when the telephone rings or when there's a knock at the door.

It's not God's problem, it's ours. It's not that God isn't doing anything, it's that we have allowed ourselves to react negatively to life's daily problems to the point where we no longer see the flower blooming and spot the miracles that are happening all around us. It's not a matter of having problems or not having problems, it's a matter of how to react to them.

**I will react positively
to my circumstances today**

Count Your Miracles Every Day

"For the Lord is good; His steadfast love endures forever, and His faithfulness to all generations."
Psalm 100:5

I believe that every human being experiences many wonderful miracles every day. The only thing is, we don't know it. We just probably don't spot them, or perhaps we have an unrealistic definition of what a miracle is.

What is a miracle? A miracle is some wonderful thing that happens to us that we can't explain, where all the odds are that it shouldn't have worked out that way, but it worked out beautifully. By all odds it should have ended up catastrophically or disastrously, but by some stroke of divine providence over which we had no control, it worked out so much better.

God is good to all of us. There are a hundred million miracles happening every day. If you can't count miracles every day, it doesn't mean God isn't doing something good for you. It means you aren't spiritually capable at that point in time of sensing the goodness that is there.

God is so good to me

Count Your Miracles Every Day

"And Christ became a human being and lived here on earth among us and was full of loving forgiveness and truth."

John 1:14

As you know, when I was 4 years old my Uncle Henry tousled my hair and said, "You're going to be a minister someday!"

Chance meetings, chance greetings, off-the-cuff remarks. This week, today, this very moment, God is trying to say something to you and that's a miracle. What is a miracle? It's when God decides to personally move into your life and do something with you.

We're aware of millions of ideas, sights, sounds, emotions and a multitude of other things each and every day.

There are fantastic hidden possibilities in them all!

Look for them.

**God is moving personally in my life
out of His great love for me**

Count Your Miracles Every Day

"You have always protected him and his home and his property from all harm."

Job 1:10

When my only son was a little boy, he learned to drive the car in the empty drive-in church through the week. He would sit in my lap, put his tiny little hands on the wheel, and unknown to him I would hold the bottom of the steering wheel. He would manipulate the curves so well and put the car right into the correct parking space, and he would say, "Didn't I do a good job, Daddy? All by myself." And I would say, "Yes, son, you sure did." But my hand was always at the bottom of the wheel.

I call that a miracle. And only God knows how many times you were spared from a crisis because He kept His hand, unseen, at the bottom of the wheel.

Count your miracles every day. Become an expert miracle spotter, and you'll have something to laugh about every day of your life!

Count your miracles every day

Count Your Miracles Every Day

*"For the Lord God is a sun and shield; he bestows
favor and honor. No good thing does the Lord
withhold from those who walk uprightly."*
                                                    Psalm 84:11

I just made a list of some of the comments I
heard people make recently. I've covered
thousands of miles this week and I've been making
notes while travelling. These are comments I have
heard people say: "An odd coincidence," was the
comment one person made. Somebody else said,
"I had a marvelous serendipity." I heard this
phrase, "A wonderful thing happened yesterday."
Another one, "You'll never guess who I ran into
today." Or, "You'll never believe what I experienced." Or, "Boy, did I hit it lucky a little while
ago." Or, "That's odd." I hear that one a lot.

And so the world calls these things coincidences,
serendipities and unexpected good things. I call
them acts of God. A hundred million miracles are
happening every day, but only those who have
the faith can spot them on life's way.

It's not odd. It's God.

Count Your Miracles Every Day

"Sing to the Lord, bless His name; tell of His salvation from day to day."

Psalm 96:2

There are miracles happening all the time. Why don't we spot them? Probably because they're not advertised. Probably because we are cybernetically and subconsciously so conditioned by negative vibrations in our impossibility-thinking society that we are no longer sensitive to see the miracles that are happening. Most people read the daily newspaper. It is almost totally a collection of all bad news. If somebody published a daily newspaper and printed all the good things that happened, they'd lose money! If you were to publish all the good things that were happening in a city or town you couldn't get by with a thin newspaper of 20 pages. It would be 12 to 18 inches thick! There are so many beautiful things happening in so many lives every day!

Beautiful things are happening every day

Count Your Miracles Every Day

"Now change your mind and attitude to God and turn to Him so He can cleanse away your sins and send you wonderful times and refreshment from the presence of the Lord."

Acts 3:19

There's another reason why we emphasize the bad instead of the good. It's because it feeds our negative emotions. You know the Bible has a great expression. It says that man is by nature conceived and born sinful. Now what does that mean? It means a great deal. It means that by nature we are out of touch with God. And when we're out of touch with God, we look for the bad instead of the good. We expect the worst instead of the best. We become cynical, skeptical and suspicious instead of trusting, hopeful and believing. So we hunger for bad news!

Look today for the "good news". That's what Gospel literally translated means—"Good News".

Find the good news in your Bible, and then in the world around you.

I am in touch with God. He helps me to look for the good.

Turn Your Mountains Into Miracles

"In my distress thou hast enlarged me, O Lord."
                                        Psalm 4:1

I happen to believe that many miracles happen to each person every day. The only problem is, most of us haven't developed the sensitivity to spot them. I'm going to suggest that if you want to find a miracle in your life, tomorrow, today or this week, and you can't find one, simply look for a problem. Or try to find a mountain, because to a Possibility Thinker every mountain is a miracle in the making.

Every mountain is a miracle in the making

Turn Your Mountains Into Miracles

"Blessed is the man who endures trial, for when he has stood the test he will receive the crown of life which God has promised to those who love Him."

James 1:12

The Rev. Pat Shaughnessy was only 25 feet from a bomb that went off at Los Angeles airport a few years ago. He was thrown 30 feet through the air, and had both his legs nearly destroyed. The right leg had to be amputated, and doctors at first held out no hope for his life. But God sped up his recovery, which a hospital spokesman termed "miraculous."

"It was not an *accident*" Pat says, "it was an *incident* in the life of a Christian. I know God was in control and directed things for my good. Through this incident, God has expanded my ministry in a wonderful way. Our reaction to the stimuli of life is based on what we believe. I believe Jesus allows everything to happen for a purpose. He can turn a mountain into a miracle. I was not the victim of that bomb blast. I was the victor."

**I am not a victim—
I am a victor through Christ**

Turn Your Mountains Into Miracles

"I call heaven and earth to witness against you that I have set before you life and death, the blessing and the curse: Therefore choose life, so that you may live, you and your children."
Deuteronomy 30:19

Two young boys were raised in the home of an alcoholic father. As they became young men, they separated from that broken home and each went his own way. Later on, a psychologist who was trying to analyze what drunkenness does to children in the home searched out those two young men. One turned out to be like his father, a hopeless alcoholic. The other one turned out to be a clean, sharp teetotaler. The counselor asked each individually the question, "Why did you become an alcoholic?" and "Why did you become a teetotaler?" They both gave the same identical answer in these words, "What else could you expect when you had a father like I did?"

It's not what happens to you in life but how you react to it that makes the difference. Every human being in the same situation has the possibilities of choosing how he will react, either negatively or positively.

It's how I react to my circumstances that makes the difference.

Turn Your Mountains Into Miracles

"But taking her by the hand he called, saying, 'Child, arise.'"

Luke 8:54

Once during a convocation for Church Growth held here on our church campus in Garden Grove, CA, a young minister was called out of a meeting for an emergency telephone call. His three and a half year old boy had fallen into a swimming pool. He was unconscious when his mother lifted him out of the pool. She applied respiration and he was revived. The whole congregation of 400 ministers had joined me in praying for that little boy.

What a great moment it was at the closing prayer during the dedication service to see the father, the mother and the boy come forward to kneel here at the front of this church. As the parents said to me later, "X-rays at the hospital showed water in the lungs. But hours later when he was x-rayed again, there was no water. The doctor said, "It's a miracle."

My life can be a miracle!

Turn Your Mountains Into Miracles

"I will lift up mine eyes to the hills, from whence cometh my help. My help cometh from the Lord, which made heaven and earth."

Psalm 121:1-2

How do you spot a miracle? Just look for a mountain. Look for a problem or a difficulty, because often the first way God reaches us is in a moment of pain.

Trouble never leaves you where it found you. It changes you, permanently. It either makes you bitter and tough and hard and cold and angry, or it'll turn you into a soft, gentle, compassionate, understanding, generous human being.

You know, if you've got a problem I predict it's the beginning of a miracle, because *what is the reason for mountains* that God lets us run into? Some mountains are there to block us so that we won't run madly ahead and get ourselves in trouble. If a mountain is there to keep us from going into enemy territory, then the mountain indeed has been turned into a miracle.

There is no gain without pain

Turn Your Mountains Into Miracles

"But the mountain shall be yours; for it is a wood, and you will cut it down: and the outgoings of it will be yours.

Joshua 17:18

I have flown around the world several times, but only once have I had to stay over for the night because of bad weather. It was in Kiev, Russia. And it was a miracle.

I was to have met with 600 Christians of the Russian underground church in Luvov. If I unwittingly led the police to them, the Christians would be imprisoned. The day before the rendezvous was to have taken place, I was with my guide in the Museum of Atheism in Leningrad when I saw there a picture of myself standing in my pulpit. It was quite a shock to me, and to my guide as well. He eyed me suspiciously.

I didn't know what to do about my contact with the Christians. But God did. My evening flight landed in Kiev enroute to Luvov, and an unexpected storm came up. Not a plane took off. God put that mountain in my path to keep me from leading His people to jail!

Often, what appear to be obstacles on our path, are really guideposts for our own good.

Consider them, pray about them. God has a better idea!

**It's not the mountain—
it's what you do with it**

The One Miracle You'll Never Forget

"Listen to advice and accept instruction, that you may gain wisdom for the future."

Proverbs 19:20

What kind of a person are you? Are you a negative, impossibility-thinking obstructionist?

Or are you a progressive possibility-thinking person?

The progressive person believes that he needs to improve. The progressive person is somebody who believes that he is not perfect; he has a blind spot, and he knows it.

Are you willing to admit that you're not perfect? That you do make some mistakes? That there are times when you have been wrong in your judgement?

The progressive person, once he knows he has a blind spot, is willing to honestly look for constructive criticism. He wants to find out what it is.

Are you willing to take that same attitude? A progressive person is anxious to get constructive criticism from his friends because he knows they really want to help him.

I am not perfect, Lord; help me to improve

The One Miracle You'll Never Forget

"And when He saw their faith, He said, 'Man, your sins are forgiven you.'"

Luke 5:20

The progressive person admits publicly his shortcomings, failings and mistakes, and he utters the sentence that more than anything else marks him now as a maturing adult. He says, "You were right, and I was wrong." He's on the edge of a miracle that will be the one miracle that he'll never forget. He's about to be changed as a person at a very deep level. And marvel of marvels, he's about to say, "I forgive you." He's about to hear the words, "You are forgiven."

I am forgiven—praise God!

The One Miracle You'll Never Forget

"If My people who are called by My name humble themselves, and pray and seek my face, and turn from their wicked ways, then I will hear from heaven, and will forgive their sins and heal their land."

II Chronicles 7:14

The forgiven person begins to suddenly change. He becomes a new person, an open person, a free person. No longer does he try to give people the impression that he's perfect. The arrogance is gone. The professorial hauteur, the pontifical pride melts away. Suddenly he stands there just another honest, humble human being who is saying to everybody, "Maybe I am the head of the History Department, but there are some aspects of history I don't understand; still I hope I can learn them." "Maybe I'm the professor of theology at the seminary, but students, there are lots of things I don't understand." Maybe he's the pastor of a church and he's saying to his people, "I really am no better than you. I have my sins and shortcomings, too. We're all trying to do the same thing—namely, improve and grow into beautiful people through whom Jesus Christ can shine." So the progressive person becomes an honest person: No more masks, no more games, no phoney claims, no false pretending.

Jesus Christ can shine through me

The One Miracle You'll Never Forget

"And through Him to reconcile all things to Himself, those on earth as well as those in Heaven, as through Him God made peace by means of the blood of His cross."

Colossians 1:20

Now the big miracle begins to happen. A bridge is built where there was no bridge. A wall is torn down where there was a barrier. Communication is restored; a fracture is mended; the polarization turns into dialogue; suspicion gives way to trust. Suddenly the miracle happens. What is it? In one word, it's *reconciliation.*

Each of us have constructed barriers or walls in our lives. It may be between a friend or a loved one. It may even be between God and yourself.

Begin to build a bridge today. Tear a stone out of the wall.

Pick up the phone, or pray to God.

But do something today to reconcile!

Communication brings reconciliation

The One Miracle You'll Never Forget

"All this is from God, who reconciled us to himself and gave us the ministry of reconciliation."
II Corinthians 5:18

What is the one miracle that is better and greater and more beautiful than all other miracles? It's reconciliation between man and God—when reconciliation takes place between a person who wasn't a believer and a God who was trying to win his or her love all the time.

Once there was a chasm between God and myself. A bridge was built, a line of communication was established, and we've got something going, the Lord and I. Reconciled to God. Forgiven of sin. I don't think anything is more beautiful than reconciliation.

Jesus is the bridge over troubled water

The One Miracle You'll Never Forget

*"For if, when we were enemies, we were
reconciled to God by the death of His Son, much
more, being reconciled, we shall be saved by His
life."*

Romans 5:10

Many years ago, our little church was split over
expansion. Many of my officers resigned their
posts and left. It was a sad day for me.

Some time ago I got a telephone call from the
wife of the treasurer. "Bob, John is very sick," she
said. "His liver is so bad, he's been in a coma
twice. You know, he's always loved you, in spite
of what happened. I was hoping you'd pray for
him."

I got on a plane and flew to Sacramento, picked
up a rental car and drove one hour to the hospital.
I found John on the fourth floor, sitting on the bed
in a bathrobe. All 6'3" of him had dwindled down
to 134 pounds. His eyes were sunken in his head,
his cheeks were hollow. He stood up, walked over
to me, we shook hands, and then we hugged each
other like two strong brothers. We had a great time
talking and praying together for two hours.
Reconciliation!

**Reconciliation—a beautiful word,
a beautiful experience**

The One Miracle You'll Never Forget

"Besides this you know what hour it is, how it is full time now for you to wake from sleep. For salvation is nearer to us now than when we first believed."

Romans 13:11

God can't do it alone. You have to cooperate. You have to respond, positively, in faith. *It takes two to make a miracle!*

Probably the greatest miracle that ever happened in your life is happening right now. You are becoming a believer. You are asking Jesus Christ to come into your life. You are ready to make a lasting, life-changing decision to become a more beautiful person. You are in the process of being saved.

Years from now you will look back at this moment and you'll say, "Wow! I hadn't planned to ever know God. I hadn't thought about reconciling myself to Him before this week. It's a miracle!"

It takes two to make a miracle

GOD'S WAY
TO THE GOOD LIFE

Commitment—The Pathway To The Good Life

"Commit your work to the Lord, then it will succeed."

                                        Proverbs 16:3

Early in my life, I made a commitment to find a place where I could spend 40 years, virtually my whole working life, in one church. It was a rare decision. Seldom do ministers approach their professional future with that kind of commitment. But I had the theory that a lifetime commitment of building, layer upon layer, would produce enormous strength. I call that the laminating principle. It is like a laminated wood beam, each layer increases the strength of the beam.

When I made a commitment to begin this church over 28 years ago, was I sure that the evolving congregation and I would always get along? No. Could I be assured that I would experience a greater growth doing that than skipping around from church to church? No.

I came here with a 40-year goal. When we reach it, we will have really accomplished something! We will have added layer upon layer, and we'll have built a great church!

Commitment to a lifetime goal doesn't limit growth. Rather, it gives you a constantly expanding emotional and intellectual power base that's deep and wide enough to support you under the shocks of life.

Lord, give me the courage that is needed to make a commitment!

Responsibility—The Runway of "No Turning Back"

"Ill-gotten gain brings no lasting happiness; right living does."

Proverbs 10:2

There are two ways to get what you need and want. One of the choices will give you self-esteem; the other will produce shame. The eighth commandment, "Thou shall not steal", has been given to us by God so we can discover the pathway to prosperity with peace of mind.

Last year Mrs. Schuller and our two daughters, Carol and Gretchen, had lunch at a little Orange County restaurant. When we came out, we were shocked to find the entire back window of our car smashed, and the broken glass was strewn over the parking lot. In broad daylight someone had pounded the window out, and stolen everything. That person took Carol's, Gretchen's and Arvella's purses. And even Gretchen's homework!

There is something very offensive about being ripped off. Theft has reached epidemic proportions in America. In fact, $20 *billion* was reported stolen last year. Robbery is negative prosperity—unsatisfying and very temporary. God has a better way!

My heart is tuned to the spirit of God. I can feel his values becoming my values!

Responsibility—The Runway of "No Turning Back"

"Whatever we do, it is certainly not for our own profit, but because Christ's love controls us now."
                                    II Corinthians 5:14

A friend of mine bought a personal jet airplane and invited me to lunch with him in Cabo San Lucas, at the tip of Baja, California. He said, "Bob, since you're a possibility thinker, I want you to take the controls of this jet.

"Now come in low," he continued, "go right between those rocks, curve and go over the bay where we'll dip the wings over the boat waiting for us."

I gulped and put my hands on the controls, following his instructions. It was incredibly simple. As easy as putting melted butter on a hot bun. I flew that plane right over the Finistera Hotel and cleanly between the rocks. It's a tremendous feeling having the power to control the direction of such a plane.

Imagine you are in a jet airplane. You're putting your hands on the controls for the first time, and you're steering this magnificent flying machine. What potential you have! Similarly, we have the same kind of directional control over our own lives.

And, oh!, what positive power we possess!

I rejoice in the vibrant, God-given power within me as I commit myself to action!

Responsibility—The Runway of "No Turning Back"

"But people who long to be rich soon begin to do all kinds of wrong things to get money, things that hurt them and make them evil-minded and finally send them to hell itself."

I Timothy 6:9

Some things you *need,* and some you *want.* God knows what they are, and He knows what's best for you. He also has a plan for you in which you can get what you need without running the risk of the shame and imprisonment that follows theft.

Every person, without exception, has the freedom to choose whether he'll follow God's plan or ignore it. Each one of us has the freedom to choose how he will steer his own life. Nobody makes that decision but *you.*

You have the power to control your life and your prosperity. You even have the power to turn your poverty into prosperity. You can get what you really need, and want, if you'll do it God's way.

I thank God for my prosperity as I act on His ideas and His riches!

Responsibility—The Runway of "No Turning Back"

"For the love of money is the first step toward all kinds of sin. Some people have even turned away from God because of their love for it, and as a result have pierced themselves with many sorrows."

I Timothy 6:10

There are two ways to get what you need and want. One is to steal. The other—the proud, honorable way—is to join in a partnership with God. He alone knows what you *need*. He knows what you *want*, and He has a plan. He tells each of us that we all have the same human rights.

The eighth commandment controls the Judaic Christian civilization. The Jewish people and the Christian church are joined hand in hand in our belief that every human being has a God-given right to possess property that the state cannot and may not confiscate. We believe everyone has the right to own a piece of property. Consequently, communism has never been compatible with the Judaic-Christian civilization.

Thank God we don't live in a communist country. Gratefully, you and I have the right to acquire property. We also have the right to produce products that fill human needs, begin our own businesses, create job opportunities, and acquire wealth.

My prosperity is in God's rich resources.

Responsibility—The Runway of "No Turning Back"

"It is better to have little and be godly than to own an evil man's wealth."

Psalm 37:16

The eighth commandment is the foundation stone upon which the whole American economic system rests. Because we have the right to earn money, possess wealth, and own property, we are able to have personal rights. If there were no property rights, there would be no personal rights!

Some think that if all property was owned by the state, all people would be treated equally. That's absolutely not true! If you do not have property rights, the state, anytime they want to, can knock on your door. They can even open that door and invade your privacy. *There are no human rights without property rights!*

God wants us to be successful—to acquire wealth, possessions and property. But He must always be placed first in our lives and above everything on earth. Prosperity in partnership with God is not only for this life, but for eternity.

God wants me to prosper. Whatever I touch, in faith, will succeed!

Responsibility—The Runway of "No Turning Back"

"Stay away from the love of money; be satisfied with what you have. For God has said, 'I will never, never fail you or forsake you.'"

Hebrews 13:5

Our responsibility toward our own prosperity is to work for your needs and wants. Don't expect someone else to provide for you. Don't wait for a handout. Don't ask the state or the county to take care of you.

If you know what you need and want, then join hands with God. He'll make it possible for you to earn it in some way. First, however, you must have the right attitude. Your attitude must indicate that you see what you have left, not what you have lost. Look to tomorrow and all that it can hold.

God can help us work our way through any situation. And in the process, no matter how tough the climb, no matter how high the mountain, no matter how difficult the struggle, when we make it, we will have that much more pride in ourselves and faith in the future.

I am ready for the success and prosperity God has for me!

Responsibility—The Runway of "No Turning Back"

"Bring all the tithes into the storehouse so that there will be food enough in my temple; if you do, I will open up the windows of heaven for you and pour out a blessing so great you won't have room enough to take it in! Try it! Let me prove it to you!"

Malachi 3:9,10

In my early years as a pastor in this church, Mrs. Schuller and I lived on a very small salary. Yet everytime it looked as though we wouldn't make it, we managed to get by until the next paycheck came. Sometimes that meant having only twenty-five or fifty cents to live on for a few days. But when the next paycheck came, I had a tremendous sense of accomplishment. We made it on what we had! And that was exciting!

We always made it because we didn't believe in stealing from God. We tithed. It was a law in the Old Testament that 10% of the fruit of one's labor went to God. And for this obedience, God poured out His blessings.

This is still true today!

Take one daring step: bring one tenth of your earnings this week to the offering plate. If you don't have the faith to do that, you won't have the faith to even try some of the ideas God wants to give you. Tithing—it's a sensational concept. Grab hold of it as if it were a jet. It may be something you've never had your hands on before, but you'll be surprised at the power it will give you in controlling your destination. God has told you His way to get what you need and want. The rest is up to you.

I will follow God's way to prosperity!

Communication—The Roadway to Success

"You must not lie."

Exodus 20:16

The ninth commandment is a positive prescription for powerful living! The eighth commandment protects property, and the ninth commandment protects truth.

If you want a truly enthusiastic life, you have to discover the secret of effective communication. None of us will succeed in business, marriage, or socially until we become skilled communicators. This commandment points us to the challenge of becoming super-successful in our interpersonal relationships.

When you learn how to communicate with people, you won't have to gossip, criticize, or lie. You won't bear false witness. Instead you'll be open and honest, and your reputation will affirm you!

Interpersonally, as well as economically, it is important that people are able to trust you. When you learn to communicate, people will believe in you. They'll know when you make big statements, you'll produce. They can count on you, depend on you, and yes—even *bank* on you.

With Jesus in me, I have the courage to be open, honest and trustworthy!

Communication—The Roadway to Success

"If you want a happy, good life, keep control of your tongue, and guard your lips from telling lies."
I Peter 3:10

Any success I've achieved in my life I owe to the five God inspired principles that I'll be sharing in the next few days. I learned them from Dr. Henry Poppen who came to our home in northwest Iowa when I was a boy and told us dashing tales of daring in Mainland China. This brave missionary captured my respect and admiration as he told of his many adventures while sharing the good news of Christ with the people of China.

Then came the great conflict between Japan and China when half a million Chinese refugees escaped to an island without shelter or food. The English government appointed Dr. Poppen to be the governor of those refugees. I asked him later how he dared to face up to the Japanese general's demand of surrender. Instead of being frightened and intimidated by him, he courageously declared that he would not surrender; and in fact, he told the general to bring soybeans to feed the people. In response to my question of his daring he replied, "Bob, I merely spoke to that Japanese general the way I talk to anybody. I have five words that I communicate by: Be *friendly, frank, fair, firm,* and *faithful.*"

I have used his advice in communicating with my family and staff and believe me, *they work!*

**By the power of Christ in me,
I am courageous!**

Communication—The Roadway to Success

"Don't use bad language. Say only what is good and helpful to those you are talking to, and that will give them a blessing."
                    Ephesians 4:29

How do you communicate effectively? First, be *friendly*. See every person with whom you must deal as a beautiful human being. There are no totally wicked, thoroughly perverse, satured evil beings. There may be some people who do terrible things, make caustic comments, or perform most dismally. But if that's the case, it is because they're afraid, insecure or frightened.

Be *friendly*. See even the most difficult people as human beings who probably have terrible problems. Believe the best about them. Expect the best from them. When you do, you'll create a mental climate where you will motivate them to become the persons you see them to be. Every human being wants to be treated with respect and dignity. Nobody wants to be pushed aside, insulted, abused or violated. So . . . be *friendly*.

**More than I want to have a friend,
I want to be a friend!**

Communication—The Roadway to Success

"Hold tightly to the pattern of truth I taught you, especially concerning the faith and love Christ Jesus offers you."

II Timothy 1:13

When you are genuinely friendly, you can move to the next stage of communication. You can be *frank.* In a very friendly way, you can address someone and say, "I think we've got a problem. Shall we be honest about it? Do you dare to talk about it? I don't know if I do. It scares me to even bring up the subject. But maybe we ought to, because it probably isn't going to go away."

Be friendly, then frank. Talk it out. You know conflict in interpersonal relationships is almost always the result of a confusion of expectations, usually on the nonverbalized level. Consequently, if you have a conflict in communications, assume the other person has misunderstood you and has a different set of expectations. You could be very frank and say, "What did you expect out of this relationship? Have I disappointed you? If so, how can I compensate for it?"

There is the danger that if you're too friendly, you won't dare to be frank. Some people are so tactful they never make contact. The courage to be skillfully frank with another comes from the deep love that only Christ can put in our hearts.

The love of God will flow through all my communications with others today.

Communication—The Roadway to Success

*"Don't criticize and speak evil about each other
If you do, you will be fighting against God's law of
loving one another."*

James 4:11

Be friendly, frank and then be *fair*. Fairness comes,
not by making accusations, not by hurling charges or
condemning statements, but by wisely using the
interrogative approach. Ask questions like, "Well, I'm
sure that you and I can learn from each other." Or, "I
would like to know why you haven't done this? You
must have a good reason for it."

Ask questions that buy time, because many
relationships need time to work themselves out. Ask
the question, "Can we take a week to think about this
and try to understand where each of us is coming
from?" Or, "Would you be willing to let it cool for
awhile and get together a week from now?"

Ask disarming questions. Questions that build up
self-dignity and self-respect. Remember, you're never
going to make progress in communications if you insult
people or put them down. Anytime you reply with a
judgment, a statement of accusation or an opinionated
formulation appraising the situation, you are immediately putting others on the defensive.

You can, however, build people up when you ask
such questions as, "Will you please tell me why you're
doing it that way? You might be right. On the other
hand, you may be wrong." That's what you call being
fair, really fair.

**Lord, give me the ability to be courteously
friendly, considerately frank
and consistently fair.**

Communication—The Roadway to Success

"Jesus said to them, 'You are truly my disciples if you live as I tell you to, and you will know the truth, and the truth will set you free.'"

John 8:32

The fourth stage of effective communication is to be *firm*. Speak from conviction. Speak from principle. Speak from integrity. Learn how to say, "I'm sorry, but this is the way I see it. I cannot violate my morality or my ethics."

And then be *faithful*. People will come to know that if you say no, it truly means you've prayed about it and are convinced your decision is the right one for you. On the other hand, if you say yes, they will know they can count on you . . . that you won't run with the hares and dash with the hounds. They will know that you are not a vague, emotionally unstable personality.

If you want to succeed in communicating, don't fall into the trap of lying, gossiping, criticizing, or condemning. Take Jesus into your heart and let Him control your thinking. If you live under the lordship of Christ and walk in prayer with Him, you are free indeed.

Once you've found this freedom, you'll have self-confidence. You'll be very *friendly! Frank! Fair! Firm!* And *faithful!*

The principles of good communication are easy to follow when Jesus is leading!

Communication—The Roadway to Success

*". . . Much is required from those to whom much
is given, for their responsibility is greater."*
                                    Luke 12:48

On my way home, returning from a trip to
Milwaukee, some friends of mine picked me up at
the airport and said, "You've got to stop and see
Miss Terry in the hospital." My schedule was
already full, but I consented, so we stopped to
make a hospital call.

I am so glad I decided to stop and see her. At
31 years of age, she is a beautiful, young, black
mother of two. But her heart is not strong enough
to keep her alive. Her only hope of survival is a
heart transplant. I prayed with her that God would
give her many years to spend with her children.
She hugged me and said, "Dr. Schuller, your
program every Sunday morning keeps my hopes
up. Thank you for what you're doing."

Miss Terry is only one of a few million people
who are counting on me and you to lift them in
a time of desperate need. There are many people
who need to be treated friendly, fairly, frankly,
firmly and faithfully. It has to start with me and *you.*

**I am sowing seeds of goodness and love,
and God will harvest them!**

Nourishment–The Only Way To Make It All The Way

"You will not covet your neighbor's house; you will not covet your neighbor's wife, or their manservant, or maidservant, or ox, or ass, or anything that is your neighbor's."

Exodus 20:17

Once I counseled a woman who was born into an extremely wealthy family. They traveled all around the world, and they were always aware of the newest toys and trinkets. The parents also gave their children the very best in other areas as well.

One day, as she was pouring out her troubled life, she said, "You know, my parents always discovered the toys before we knew they existed. They always bought us gifts before we knew we wanted them. I have never wanted anything. I wish there was something that I wanted and couldn't have. It must be exciting to want something, to have to wait for it, to dream that maybe someday I could have it, and then probably get it. But I've never had such an experience."

I hope there is something you want that you don't have. We grow through the experience of dealing with our wants. How do you handle your wants? Negatively or positively? This final commandment warns that if you handle your wants negatively, you'll really be in trouble. Coveting, you see, is negatively working out our acquisition fantasies.

God will help me to deal with my desires in a positive way

Nourishment–The Only Way To Make It All The Way

"Wherever your treasure is, there your heart and thoughts will be also."
Luke 12:34

As a sophomore in Western Theological Seminary, I'd completed my undergraduate work and was doing my theological work. In a year or two I would be graduating as an ordained clergyman. I sensed a tremendous, instinctive, impulsive, divine dream to do something great with the one life I had to live. I didn't want to live my life and then die without making a contribution to anyone or anything. For some reason I wanted a job challenging enough that it would require all my energies and faith.

So, privately, I asked myself, "What would be the most significant ministry I could have?" That question led to the next, "What is the biggest church?" I began looking at the biggest churches in America and believed my goal should be to pastor at one of those churches someday.

But then I wondered, "If I ever did acquire the position I wanted, would I be big enough to handle the job?" It would be terrible to be given an opportunity to hold an important job only to discover I wasn't a match for the mountain.

The answer was not to turn away from the climb— but to trust totally in the promise of God's great and generous flow of grand ideas!

Lord, lead me to the thoughts and dreams that will make my life count!

Nourishment—The Only Way To Make It All The Way

"Be delighted with the Lord. Then he will give you all your heart's desires."

Psalm 37:4

At one point in pursuit of my dream, I was dangerously close to approaching my whole future with a covetous mental attitude. I prayed for guidance, and God gave me a dream which was the positive fulfillment of the tenth commandment. The dream was this: "Schuller, you want a big church. You want a big job. You want to do something worthwhile. You want to make a significant contribution. Then go out and start from scratch. Talk to one person and help that person. Help another and another until finally you bring these believers together and thereby build a Christian community—a new little church. At first it will be only a tiny little church, but the next year you do a little better job, and your church will grow as large as I want it to. The only thing you should covet is improving your old record."

So my wife and I came to California with $500. We'd decided to do the best job we could with one person, then two, five, ten and twenty. If it turned out to be a church . . . great. If it becomes a great church . . . wonderful! My prayer is, "Lord, don't let it get any bigger than you and I can handle together."

Thank you, God, for the mountains in my life that you and I are turning into miracles!

Nourishment–The Only Way To Make It All The Way

"What profit is there if you gain the whole world—and lose eternal life? What can be compared with the value of eternal life?"
                                        Matthew 16:26

How do you fulfill your wants and needs? By realizing the solution is not material, but spiritual. Many people miss out on the joys of life because they think they lack things that others have.

Things do not bring ultimate fulfillment. Materialism does not bring happiness. What do I mean by materialism? Seeking emotional fulfillment in *things.* Which means, if you're afraid, you buy a gun. If you're guilty, you send flowers or candy. If you're bored, you drink too much or spend money in order to put stimulation in life. Many people find these temporary solutions to their problems, but *emotional fulfillment will not come from a material source.* Emotional fulfillment only comes from an emotional source. And God is the ultimate source of our total being.

If you want courage, confidence, aspiration, excitement, enthusiasm and vitality for life, get it through spiritual nourishment.

**Fulfillment comes from knowing
Jesus through His word!**

Nourishment–The Only Way To Make It All The Way

"For I can do everything God asks me to with the help of Christ who gives me the strength and power."

Philippians 4:13

Materialism is shallow nourishment. The happiness it brings cannot last. When you've bought the house and the last piece of furniture, after while, you don't even notice it anymore.

I learned this from Richard Neutra, one of the great architects of our century. When we retained him to build our first church building he said, "You know, one of the problems with buildings is that they are things, and things go out of style. Because things don't grow, they don't change. They are static and people become bored with them."

"But," he added, "I have a solution to that problem. People will never get bored with the buildings I'll build because they'll see right through them. They'll see the sky and the trees. Some days the sky will be a drab gray. Other days it will be a bright blue. At nighttime, the stars and the moon will be visible. The building will be dynamic, exciting, and always changing."

The earth, the universe, the galaxies confirm to me the genius and power of my Creator!

Nourishment–The Only Way To Make It All The Way

"Love does no wrong to anyone. That's why it fully satisfies all of God's requirements. It is the only law you need."

Romans 13:10

What are you coveting? I believe what you really want at the deepest level is joy. You get it through love and through faith. Jesus Christ is the fulfillment of the law, which means He is the fulfillment of the Ten Commandments. If you have the power and the life of the risen Christ within you, and if the Holy Spirit possesses your mind and permeates your emotions, you'll have everything you could possibly want. You'll have love and care about people as persons, not as things to manipulate, possess or use.

There's no way water can flow through a tube without leaving its moist remembrance behind. There is no way a fragrant flower can bloom without leaving a perfume in the air, and there's no way for Jesus Christ to come into your mind and heart and life and flow through you without leaving a beautiful feeling behind. You'll feel completely satisfied, and you won't want anything else.

When you love people with Christ's love, you'll have your immediate reward.

Christ is the fulfillment of the law and the fulfillment of love!

Nourishment–The Only Way To Make It All The Way

"The Kingdom of God is not just talking; it is living by God's power."

I Corinthians 4:20

Christ is the fulfillment of the law, and He gives you love and faith—fantastic faith! The kind that does not *covet,* but *carves* out your own dream. He gives you the faith to head for the promised land—your impossible dream. Risking the possibility of failure, you take the plunge and make it! And end up with the pride of *earnership,* which is even more fulfilling than the pride of *ownership.*

The tenth commandment wraps the other up. When you find emotional fulfillment, you don't need to covet. You won't be tempted to steal or commit adultery. You'll dare to be honest! Everything comes together when you find emotional fulfillment in a beautiful relationship with God through Jesus Christ.

Christ gives love. Christ gives faith. Christ gives dreams, and then the courage to hang in there and to believe those dreams will come true! He gives the hope that makes us immune to coveting.

He has a dream for you today. I don't know what it is, but pray it through. Seek His will. Discover His plan, because He wants your dreams to come true, too!

With God's help I will face my dream and see what great things He has planned for me!

A Positive Attitude–The Gateway To The Greatway

"Now you can really serve God; not in the old way, mechanically obeying a set of rules, but in the new way, with all your hearts and minds."
                                    Romans 7:6

Dr. Karl Menninger, a leading psychiatrist of our century, once said, "Attitude is more important than facts." The facts may be that you are facing the biggest mountain of your life. However, your attitude is more important than the mountain you face!

When we started this ministry years ago, with a lack of money, members, and property, we held our first service in a drive-in theater. There, with my wife and my Lord, Jesus Christ, I delivered a message entitled, "I Have a Dream." My dream, I said, was to build one of the greatest churches in the world. I didn't mean buildings that could be built, I meant a *real* church. A collection of people committed to loving the unlovely, encouraging the discouraged, and putting hope into the hearts of people who are ready to give up on life. A real church is where Jesus Christ is alive, incarnate, through the Holy Spirit in human beings.

Are you facing a mountain today?

Your dream can lift you to its peak.

I can feel your spirit, Lord, active and alive in your church!

A Positive Attitude–The Gateway To The Greatway

"Blessed is the person who trusts in the Lord and has made the Lord his or her hope and confidence. You are like a tree planted along a riverbank, with its roots reaching deep into the water."
Jeremiah 17:7,8

When our church was just starting I did some traveling to clarify what kind of mission God would want to perform through us. I went around the world and saw that there wasn't a significant corner of the world that didn't already have missionaries operating in it. So we prayed, and God gave us the dream. The dream was this:

"Schuller, half of the people in the United States of America never step into any church. They may play golf, sleep-in, or watch television, but many do not go to church."

So God gave us a very unique mission to bring a positive hope-filled and Christ-centered church service into the homes, hospitals, and prisons across America. This was our dream, and I asked for help. First, God's help. Then your help. And as a team, united to make a better world, we have found many needs and filled them. Many hurts and healed them. And continue to spread the love of Christ through this great ministry.

Trust in the Lord...be willing to hear his call, and move to his calling.

My faith is being tested daily, but I know God is guiding me!

A Positive Attitude–The Gateway To The Greatway

"For we walk by faith, not by sight."
                                    II Corinthians 5:7

The dream of having a large group of committed Christians has come true. *Hour of Power* is seen in 160 cities in the United States as well as in Korea, the Philippines, Germany, and the non-English-speaking countries where there are U.S. military bases. The Hour of Power has the world's largest Sunday morning audience of any church at worship. In America alone, this television program has the largest audience of any televised preacher. That's good news!

The challenge is there are still millions and millions of people we are not reaching. About two million people attend this church service by television every week. In addition there are 90 million who are, gratefully, in their own churches. But there are 120 million other people who don't attend church either in person or via television.

Sometimes a dream looks so big, it seems impossible. And if left to ourselves, it might be unachievable. But we know someone greater, someone who puts the seemingly impossible dreams into our minds. That someone is Jesus Christ. He not only gives us the dream, but also stays with us each step of the way until we have accomplished it!

When my faith seems weak, I keep trusting and believing for I know that with God all things are possible!

A Positive Attitude–The Gateway To The Greatway

"Those who trust in the Lord are steady as Mount Zion, unmoved by any circumstance."
                                        Psalm 125:1

Today I have a *new* dream. After spending much time in intensive prayer, God has given me this dream—to reach the point where one out of every ten unchurched persons in the United States will be tuned to the Hour of Power every Sunday. Then, God willing, two out of every ten. Then three!

When I accepted the call to start this church, there was nothing. Eventually we had 200 members. The church grew and grew until we needed a larger building, then an even larger one, until it was necessary to build the Crystal Cathedral. With its completion, pressures have come to me to pursue other avenues of Christian ministry. If I accepted them, I would have to resign my present position.

However, I have made a new commitment. Barring death or physical incapacitation, I will spend the remainder of my fruitful years serving as the pastor of this church and as the spokesman for this ministry on nation-wide television. My attitude will be one of gratitude. And I will follow the dream my Lord has given me.

What dreams do you hold today?

Already I feel confident as I recognize the Lord is working in my life!

A Positive Attitude–The Gateway To The Greatway

"In everything you do, put God first, and he will direct you and crown your efforts with success."
Proverbs 3:6

Norman Vincent Peale, my dear friend, is still preaching at the age of 83, and really "blowing them out of the water" in Marble Collegiate Church in New York City. I run five miles every morning. Physically, I feel great. Mentally, I feel terrific. The next 25 years, the next quarter century, between the ages of 55 and 80, do you know what you and I could do? We can actually change America's thinking. Indeed, we can!

I had the great honor of being asked to deliver a speech at a major Jewish community function. Of all the great rabbis in this country that they could have picked, they chose me–a protestant pastor! When I took the platform, they applauded the ministry of this Crystal Cathedral and said, "When your congregation built that cathedral, you inspired all of us to dream dreams and climb towering mountains."

Who do you look to for inspiration?...and who is looking to you?

Make your source God almighty, and you'll be a light to all those you meet.

Today I feel the exhilaration of climbing God's mountain!

A Positive Attitude—The Gateway To The Greatway

"Let this mind be in you, which was also in Christ Jesus."

Philippians 2:5

A positive attitude is the winning difference. When we decided to start what is now known as the Crystal Cathedral and the Hour of Power, churches were on the decline. People said, "Schuller, this is the worst time to start in a business that's going out of style." *The worst of the times are the best of the times, if God is leading.*

Do you know why we have been put on this earth?

To be witnesses to God's power.

The challenge is to keep the dream alive.

What dreams would you have today if you knew you could not fail? If you knew you'd have the time, talent and the money—what dream would you "go for" tomorrow?

Somebody said, "These are economically tough times." However, God has always called me to start at the worst of times.

The worst of times are the best of times, if you have a positive attitude.

I repeat: The worst of times are the best of times, if God is leading.

Climbing the mountain may be difficult, but from the peak I see greater possibilities!

A Positive Attitude–The Gateway To The Greatway

"Now change your mind and attitude to God and turn to him so he can cleanse away your sins and send you wonderful times of refreshment from the presence of the Lord."

Acts 3:19

In the past, God has found people who had the sources to give us the help we needed. They were people I didn't even know. Today I see a mountain again, but I thank God for mountains to climb. It's the mountains that provide us with the opportunity to witness to the world of God's power.

Everyone faces mountains. And everyone has to decide whether they will climb them or not. Some do not choose to go through all the work, effort, strain, sweat and tears. That's the very question I have wrestled with. Because other opportunities for service with less pressure and less demands have been very tempting. Then I run into people in airports and hotels and hear comments like, "If it hadn't been for your television program, I wouldn't have the faith I have today. You know, you pointed me in the right direction, and now I go to a church and I've accepted Jesus."

The mountain is worth the climb if we're in God's will!

A Positive Attitude–The Gateway To The Greatway

"When someone becomes a Christian a brand new person is inside. A new life has begun!"

II Corinthians 5:17

Ken Clissold, a member of the Hour of Power congregation, shared the following story.

"The possibility thinking theme that flows through this ministry became, for me, a solid foundation when it was discovered suddenly that I have cancer. The witnesses of people like B. J. Thomas, John Crean, and Art Linkletter helped me to get through this crisis. Through people like them, I developed a positive attitude that smoothed the way for the acceptance of the Lord in my life.

"You simply can't imagine the shock that day when the doctors told me I had leukemia. Their announcement came just days after I had quit my position. The guy I had been relying on—me—was now sick in bed. Who would help me?

"As Dr. Schuller has suggested many times on his television service, I found the Lord accepting of my confessions; and I also found a smiling, warm welcome from the family of God at my local church."

Grab hold today of the omnipotence of God.

I am continuously being changed through the power of Christ!

A Positive Attitude–The Gateway To The Greatway

"Many say that God will never help us. Prove them wrong, O Lord, by letting the light of your face shine down upon us."

Psalm 4:6

Ken Clissold's story continues:
"Then I faced a bone marrow transplant, a corrective procedure whereby they take healthy bone marrow from someone in my family and transplant it into my body, since my own cancerous bone marrow was chemically destroyed. Therein, the new healthy bone marrow starts to grow, rejuvenating my life.

"The doctors explained the transplant process, but they cautioned that the specifications were so rigid, so tight, that it precluded anybody who had ever had hepatitis. The donor must have identical blood and tissue types. We put our trust in the Lord and tested my sons, my brother. We couldn't believe what we found—a perfect match in my father, Vern. Father and son blood and tissue matches only occur one in 100 cases. It was a miracle solution for me! But one I may never have had the opportunity to even find if it had not been for the trust in God that led to my positive attitude!

My prayer is simply that more people will come to know the Lord through the Hour of Power. It worked for my benefit, and I would like others to have the same chance."

Lord, how great it is to know that we are being used to glorify you!

DISCOVER
AN ENTHUSIASTIC
NEW LIFE TODAY

Live Right

"And the angel spoke to the women. 'Don't be frightened!' he said. 'I know you are looking for Jesus, who was crucified, but he isn't here! For he has come back to life again, just as he said he would.'"

Matthew 28:5

Jesus Christ is alive! Accept it! Believe it! Know it! Then ask yourself, *what does it mean to me?*

It's not "new" news but "old" news. Better to have old news that has been tested, tried and proven for two thousand years than some new-fangled idea that may sound exciting and progressive but has not yet passed the test of time. The old news I have for you is that Jesus Christ is alive and through His Spirit He can come into a human life and change a personality. It is an established fact that multiplied millions of people have found mental and emotional health and wholeness through a dynamic Christian relationship with their Lord, and *it can happen to you!*

Glory Hallelujah!
Jesus Christ is alive today!

Live Right

"Commit your way to the Lord; trust in him, and he will act."

Psalm 37:5

Would you be content to live the rest of your life the way you're living right now?

If you'd like to live a more exciting, enthusiastic, confident, expectant life, then I have help for you!

When you think about yourself, trouble grows. When you think about Christ, *trouble goes!*

Jesus Christ is alive, and He knows you! He cares about you! He cares about what's happening in your life—your dreams, your work, your marriage, your family and your job! *Yes, He does!*

The glory of the resurrection is that Jesus Christ got His body out of the way, liberated Himself so that through the power of the Holy Spirit He could return again to live in millions of lives all over the world, to help human beings in their lives and as they move on into eternity.

I feel Christ's come-alive-power in my life right now!

Live Right

"He fulfills the desires of those who reverence and trust him; he hears their cries for help and rescues them."

Psalm 145:19

What can Jesus Christ do for you? I submit He can do for you what He is doing for me. This is my testimony:

Christ can *reach you* wherever you are.

He can *redeem* you, no matter what you've done.

He can *release* you, no matter how trapped you feel.

He can *reveal* your possibilities, even though you've never understood them before.

He can *reassure* you of your worth, of the meaning and purpose of life, and of your eternal destiny—so that you'll never be afraid again!

**I am one with Christ.
I willingly follow Him!**

Live Right

"Your body is a temple of the Holy Spirit."
I Corinthians 6:19

The Bible is filled with many statements indicating that our relationship to God vitally affects our human energy output. And obviously, energy levels differ from one person to another. The question I ask is, "Why?"

Now of course, there is such a thing as having a healthy body. If you don't eat right, if you don't exercise right, if you neglect your physical body, you can expect your energy output to suffer drastically.

For the past few years I've been on a physical fitness program and have run six to seven miles each morning. I feel great and have learned that when I'm too tired to endure physical exercise, the way to get more energy is to do it anyway! After I've run about two miles, strength comes. After three, I have more energy. And after four, I'm ready to go!

Many people do not have a high energy level because they are not willing to pay the price in discipline over their own bodies. If you keep your body in good shape, the Holy Spirit can live there. The Holy Spirit then becomes your source of tremendous emotional (or psychic) energy!

**My body carries the Holy Spirit of God.
My physical well-being is important!**

Live Right

"That out of his glorious, unlimited resources he will give you the mighty inner strengthening of his holy spirit."

Ephesians 3:16

On a television talk show, the interviewer asked me why I always seemed enthusiastic. I replied that I'm basically a very joyful, happy person. He pressed, "Yes, but is it reasonable to expect that most people can be happy the way you say you are?" I answered, "I think so, I really do! I believe if you live right, think right, pray right, love right, give right and act right, you can't help but be bubbling over with energy and enthusiasm! *Only the authentic, honest person can be enthusiastic!*

Most people who aren't enthusiastic probably aren't living right. Because they're not honest, they're afraid they might spill the beans. They have to be careful of what they say. If you live such an open, clean life that you don't have to be careful of what you say, you'll be surprised how enthusiastic you can get! And enthusiasm produces energy!

The first key to high energy output is to *live right!* If you live right, you'll welcome the Holy Spirit into your life.

I am changing! I am in the process of becoming an even better person!

Love Right

"In all things I have shown you that by so toiling one must help the weak, remembering the words of the Lord Jesus, how he said, 'It is more blessed to give than to receive.'"

Acts 20:35

When the Holy Spirit enters your life, you'll start loving right. Love is an energy-producing force!

When you really love people, you get excited about them, and you want to help them. You get enthused about the projects that help people who are hurting, and this is what produces the energy!

God reveals to you some of the many wonderful things to do in this world, and you can't help but get excited! Then you'll forget about yourself, and you'll think about others who have problems. And in helping them, you become energized and blessed!

Many people who aren't enthusiastic probably aren't loving right. They're angry inside with people. If you fight battle thoughts all day, you can expect to suffer battle fatigue at night."

Only one life will soon be passed.
Only what's done for Christ will last.

Love Right

"Commit everything you do to the Lord. Trust him to help you do it and he will."

Psalm 37:5

In a meeting someone asked, "Why is it that some people have more energy than others?" One negative-thinking person spoke up, "It's all a matter of glands. Some people have energetic genes." And she pointed out that the endocrine glands are mostly responsible for rushing the adrenalin into the blood. I said, "But what stimulates the glands to activate the adrenalin?" And she said, "What? All of us have basically the same glands. The difference is that some people's glands don't get stimulated, so they don't put out energy." I replied, "It's more a matter of the blands than of the glands."

By that I meant bland living, not too spiced up, not too exciting, dull, mediocre, ho-hum. *Energy is more a matter of the blands than it is of the glands!*

Find something you can give your soul and heart to and get excited about, and you'll live on a high energy level. Love Jesus. Love yourself. Love others! And you won't be able to stop the stream of enthusiasm that will flow through you.

I rejoice in the vibrant, God-given power within me as I commit myself to action!

Love Right

*"You have given me your salvation as my shield.
Your right hand, O Lord, supports me; your
gentleness has made me great."*

Psalm 18:35

A hundred times every day God reaches out to
you, but you may not recognize him as God! You
may think it's just a man, woman, event or
circumstance, but it's God reaching out to *you*. A
thought, an impulse, an emotion, a feeling, an
idea—God reaching out to you.

You may suffer from a low self-esteem. We all
do at times. But, he wants to redeem you. He
wants to tell you that you're not as bad as you
think you are!

You need that redemption.

You need forgiveness.

God wants to redeem you in order to reveal to
you possibilities that are locked up inside of you.
The possibilities for a meaningful life, a joyful life,
a courageous life, a happy and enthusiastic life!
The possibilities of really living happily with your
fellow human beings are locked up inside of you.
He reaches out to redeem you in order to reveal
and release your possibilities for living and loving.

**I recommit myself to all of God's great
possibilities for me today!**

Love Right

"I am your God. I will strengthen you; I will help you; I will uphold you with my victorious right hand."

Isaiah 41:10

Michelangelo worked on forty-four statues in his life, but he only finished fourteen of them. We are familiar with the ones he completed—David in Florence Square, the Pieta, and Moses, to mention a few. But the thirty he never finished are very interesting, too.

In a huge chunk of marble is sculptured an elbow, the beginning of a wrist; but the rest of the man is still locked up in marble. On another piece, the leg is out, thigh, knee, calf, heel, ankle, toes, but the rest of the body is still frozen in marble. It will never come out.

I remember seeing these in a museum in Italy, and the thought struck me, "Of all the tragedies in life, the greatest one is for a person to live and die and never know what his possibilities were." Jesus Christ does not want that to happen. He *reaches* out to each of us so that he can *redeem* us. Then he *reveals* and *releases* our possibilities!

Thank you, Lord, for releasing the possibilities within me!

Love Right

"I can do all things through Christ who strengthens me."

Philippians 4:13

Your relationship with God is a vital factor in your own human energy level. The love that can flow from Him through us can cause an incredible interest and excitement in our lives.

Some time ago a friend of ours, Don Sutton, who was then the ace Los Angeles Dodger pitcher, was here and told us how every professional athlete looks for the edge. "Because," he said, "to really be a great success all you have to do is be just a little better than everybody else. It's that simple. All you need is the edge on the competition. And Jesus Christ gives me the winner's edge!"

And He does! Because God produces that dynamic flow of love which turns into enthusiastic energy!

**God fills me with strength and enthusiasm.
He makes me a winner!**

Love Right

"God is love, and anyone who lives in love is living with God and God is living in him. And as we live with Christ, our love grows more perfect."
                                                        I John 4:16,17

Physical energy, of course, is a matter of keeping your body in good shape by exercising and eating correctly. But we require not only physical, but also spiritual exercise. If a person is healthy, he's a whole person—physical and spiritual, so your relationship with God definitely affects your enthusiasm and energy.

How does that work? If you have a close relationship with your loving God, you're constantly excited! That excitement is a dynamic, natural enthusiasm which produces energy! That enthusiasm and energy bursts out of you in the form of loving others.

Talk to God today. Receive His forgiveness and love. Then take the time to either call a friend or send a note of appreciation to someone and spread the glow of His love.

Today is the day to speak of the love I have in my heart—for God, my family and my friends!

Love Right

"And whatever you do, do it with kindness and love."

                                        I Corinthians 16:14

Lord, make me an instrument of Thy peace.
Where there is hatred, let me sow love;
Where there is injury, pardon;
Where there is doubt, faith;
Where there is despair, hope;
Where there is darkness, light;
Where there is sadness, joy;
O Divine Master, grant that I may not so much seek
to be consoled, as to console;
to be understood, as to understand;
to be loved, as to love.
For it is in giving, that we receive;
It is in pardoning, that we are pardoned;
It is in dying, that we are born to eternal life.

                    Amen
                    St. Francis of Assisi

**I feel the power of God's love active within
me, soothing, healing and blessing me!**

Think Right

"In God we live and move and have our being."
Acts 17:28

Possibility thinking is not a pollyanna philosophy that ignores the reality of problems. Rather, it sees every problem being pregnant with possibilities. Problems turn me on! I don't think anything would be more dull or boring than if I had no problems!

Several times in this ministry we've experienced growth-restricting problems. We've needed more seating, more rooms, more money! These problems excite me *because every problem is an opportunity*. It's an opportunity for us to think bigger and reach higher. I don't believe we would ever grow unless God pushed us into it.

William James said, "You have enormous untapped powers that you probably will never tap, because most people never run far enough on their first wind to ever find out they've got a second."

Every adversity hides a beautiful possibility!

Think Right

"Be glad for all God is planning for you. Be patient in trouble, and prayerful always."
                                        Romans 12:12

Robert Ardrey put it this way, "Every human being has three deep needs—the need for identity, the need for security and the need for stimulation." But these deep inner needs oftentimes conflict with each other. If I were to ask you which one you would pick as your deepest need, what would you say? Most people would opt for security. In other words, they want to be sure they are secure, physically and emotionally, in their interpersonal relations, in their jobs, and in their finances. Security would be number one with most people.

But the road that is marked SECURITY is a cul-de-sac that ends with a big sign saying BOREDOM. If you achieve ultimate security, you will achieve ultimate boredom. The only way to escape boredom is to expose yourself to the stimulation of some risk, some adventure or some mountain.

I've discovered in my life that possibility thinking produces energy, because it helps me to escape from the road of security, and it commits me to the road of stimulation.

**My life is an adventure with God.
I am not afraid!**

Think Right

"When God's children are in need, you be the one to help them out."

Romans 12:13

Years ago my wife and I had a dream of a church with 6,000 members. We determined that many people would be necessary to teach Sunday School, call on the sick in the hospital, and to run a 24-hour telephone counseling service. And we thought it would probably take us forty years to build up a church of 6,000 members, so we planned to win 150 members a year. Then in forty years, we would probably retire, leaving behind a great work that would continue to be a throbbing heart of love in the heart of this country.

So that was our dream. I did not yet know, however, that Alfred North Whitehead principle, "Great dreams of great dreamers are never fulfilled, they are always transcended." I also didn't know that great dreams of great dreamers are God's dreams. And I didn't realize that God is always dreaming much bigger than I am because I usually want to play it safe. Even though I want stimulation, I want security, too. So I don't allow myself to dream so big that it becomes reckless. Even though I may try to keep my dreams smaller, God's dreams are bigger. What happened to my dream proved that. After only twenty years, we had surpassed our original plan and thinking. But we didn't eliminate problems, we inherited bigger ones!

**I want to be a great dreamer, Lord,
give me your dreams!**

Think Right

"For with God, nothing is impossible."
                                        Matthew 17:20

At Hope College I learned a wonderful principle, "Don't do something great, too many people already are. Only do something that excels." Excellence produces excitement. Excitement produces energy. Energy creates momentum. And momentum makes things happen!

Your days can be filled with happiness, thrilling excitement and youthful enthusiasm if you will learn to *think possibilities.* Most unhappiness and despair come from problem thinking. When you focus on problems, you are defeated. But when your attention is on the possibilities that accompany any problem, you're on the road to success!

Write down some problems in your life. Then make a list of all the possibilities surrounding that problem. Let your imagination run wild. Only your moral and ethical principles will limit you. Legal questions and money problems will not constrict the flow of your creative ideas.

I enter this day with high expectations and a happy heart, for with God nothing is impossible!

Think Right

"All things are possible to him who believes!"
                                                    Mark 9:23

God wants to pour out His abundance, but He doesn't give His riches to small-thinking people. He only gives it to those who believe big!

Great things are going to happen. Great miracles are about to happen. You may not know how, but keep believing.

When you think this way, you become energized! Some people are fatigued because they have no dreams. They would rather play it safe. They don't want to get involved, or take chances. They certainly don't want to run the risk of failure. And so rather than think big, they play it safe and consequently become dull! Possibility thinkers are never boring! *Because every time they've got a big problem, they know they are on the edge of a miracle!*

**All things work together for good,
because God works and I work!**

Think Right

"The things which are impossible with men are possible with God."

Luke 18:27

Your creative energies must be directed at a serious objective. There must be some deep inner concern which gets the creative energy started and keeps it going.

Only when your subconscious mind deeply believes the mind-bending project to be very, very important will the hidden powers slumbering deep in the dark regions of the unconscious rise up and awaken your creative conscious.

Some years ago I experienced an example of this potential principle. A group of us were discussing the serious illness of a mutual friends whose heart was failing fast. I recalled at the time the comment of a famous heart surgeon who said, "The invention of an artificial heart was impossible because it would require an unfailing, permanent power-generating source."

Someone said, "Why not keep the power source outside the chest cavity and simply change batteries regularly?" Although we didn't know it then, we had just described the eventual solution to that "impossible" problem! If you tune in to God's ideas, your problems can be solved. Your dreams can come true!

I abide in a constant flow of God's abundance circulating in and through my life and my plans!

Think Right

"You will keep on guiding me all my life with your wisdom and counsel."

Psalm 73:24

Once you have spotted what appears to be an opportunity, don't plunge recklessly ahead without asking sensible questions. Success-test your opportunities. Challenge all positive ideas by asking success-spotting, possibility-measuring, opportunity-testing questions:

1. Will this project fill a vital human need? Is it practical and will it help people who are hurting? How does your project measure up?

2. Will this project inspire people? Other people are attracted to the individual or the project that inspires and uplifts the heart and the human spirit. Your project may help you most, but will your success inspire and uplift others?

3. Can you do this project in an outstanding way? Excellence is a vital key to success. Can your project be both monumental and instrumental?

4. Is your solution pace-setting? Almost anything can be done differently and better. And when God is involved in your project, it deserves to be pace-setting!

**God is opening new ways to me.
My future is bright!**

Give Right

"Give, and it will be given to you. A good measure, pressed down, shaken together and running over, will be poured into your lap. For the measure you give will be the measure you get back.

Luke 6:38

Psychiatric observations and studies have indicated that nine-tenths of all fatigue among sedentary people is psychological and emotional. And that means it is theological, because you cannot divide psychology from theology. You cannot take the human soul and slice it into sections such as the brain, emotion, soul and mind. Sectionalism is improper if the whole human being is involved.

I have always had tremendous energy, but I don't think that I genetically have more energy than other people. Some people are tired because they're afraid they're going to get tired. Because they're afraid they're going to get tired, they don't spend their energy since they want to save it. Saving energy produces fatigue. If you don't have energy, the best way to get it is to *give* it out!

God is the cosmic source of all spiritual energy. When we are close to God and in tune with Him, we tap the source of energy.

I feel a growing generosity within me. I want to share all that God has given me!

Give Right

"And the measure you give will be the measure you get."

Matthew 7:2

Emerson said, "The world belongs to the energetic." And Sir Thomas Buxton put it this way, "The longer I live, the more deeply I'm convinced that what makes the difference between one man and another, the great and the insignificant, is energy, that invincible determination, a purpose that once formed nothing can take away. This energetic quality will do anything that is meant by God to be done in this world, and no talent, training, opportunity, or circumstance will make any man a man without it."

Energy is inside of you, but you have to prime the pump. What you get is what you give! Or, you can turn it around and it still holds true: What you give is what you'll get!

That's a universal principle. What you give will be returned in proportion. If you need love, *give* love. If you need money, *give* money. And if you need energy, *give* energy! *Remember, what you give is what you'll get!*

I sing a song of thanksgiving for all I have and all I can give!

Give Right

"Give as freely as you have received!"
                                                    Matthew 10:8

One morning I opened my eyes, and it was still black outdoors. I had no idea what time it was until I heard our clock . . . 5 am! "I'm still tired," I thought, "and I know I won't get back to sleep now." (What a negative thought! If you think you won't go back to sleep, naturally you won't!) So I had a battle with myself on the pillow. And then I thought, "If I want energy, the best way to get it is to go running." Actually I was too tired to run, which was only proof of the fact that that was exactly what I had to do!

So I jumped out of bed, got my running suit on and started running off into the hills. Everything went fine until, in the blackness, I turned down the wrong road, and for the first time I got lost running. I simply reached a dead-end, turned around and found myself home exactly 65 minutes after I started out. As I took my shower, I realized that the blood was in every corner of my skin. I was more energetic than ever! *I got energy by giving energy!*

**I receive abundant energy
when I give abundant energy!**

Give Right

"Never be lazy in your work but serve the Lord enthusiastically."

Romans 12:11

At a convention in Miami, Florida, one of the most powerful senators in the United States, whose name is a household word, delivered his speech right after I delivered mine. I thanked him for his words, because it was a great speech.

But even more than that, I was so impressed with this man's tremendous energy. I would say he's in his 60's, and not long ago he battled cancer. Still he bounded up that stage with energy, and he spoke for 55 minutes with energy.

Energy is not a matter of age—it's attitude! It's not a matter of general health, because I've seen people who have had major surgery, or battled cancer, and they've got loads of energy!

Do you need energy? Give it, and you'll get it. Put it out, and you'll end up with more than you used! It's really true! Try it for yourself.

**Energy is not a matter of age—
it's a matter of attitude!**

Give Right

*"For it is God who is at work within you, giving
you the will and power to achieve His purpose."*
                                        Philippians 2:13

If you need more energy it probably means you
need more faith! In a close relationship with God,
you will dream great dreams and attempt great
things. Anybody who lives and moves in the will
of God is going to be a high-energy person.

If you aren't energetic enough on your job, for
instance, probably you're not giving it enough.
You're probably reporting in as late as you can,
checking out as quickly as possible, and doing as
little as necessary while you're there. Obviously in
that kind of situation you're not going to be
enthused. And enthusiasm is energy! The word
enthusiasm is made up of en-theos—*in God.*

Is Friday the best day of the week of your week?
Do you begin to get a bit of energy Friday evening,
more energy Saturday, and plenty of pep
Saturday night? Sunday you feel good, but
Monday morning, when you go back to work, you
feel tired again? It means that you have to bring
Christ into your life and apply your faith to your
job so that you turn your job into a ministry! Begin
by *giving*—give your life to God, and you will
generate enthusiasm and energy!

**I abide in God's abundance
of enthusiasm and energy!**

Give Right

"We should make plans counting on God to direct us."

Proverbs 16:9

Once in a very important meeting, one of the lawyers became very upset. I was shocked. I could tell in that kind of mental climate with such negative vibrations that if I stayed there, I'd be fatigued in ten minutes; and I didn't want to waste my energy. I said something to this effect: "When you are able to address yourselves in positive terms and with enthusiasm in calm and reflective minds, I will be happy to rejoin the assembly."

With that I made a hasty exit. I could feel fatigue in the room because of the negative vibrations from the cantankerous, negative-thinking lawyer.

When I returned a few minutes later, the lawyer was storming out; (Miracles do happen!) but the quibbling and quarrelling started again with the remaining group. I made a suggestion which I hoped would be positive bait, and it worked! They began to discuss the project that brought them together. As they started talking about it, they started dreaming. They got excited, then enthusiastic! When they started discussing their ideas, energy came back. What a transformation took place in that room!

I am tuned to the Spirit of God! His dreams are becoming my dreams!

Give Right

"Happy are all who search for God, and always do his will."

Psalm 119:2

Do you want enthusiasm and energy? Then remember; power comes through positive and negative wires. Pull away from anything that would produce anxiety, fear, anger or guilt! And draw to anything that would produce power to dream dreams and get involved in projects and get excited!

Some people use an enormous amount of energy resisting God's Holy Spirit when He tries to move into their lives. And what happens? *God stays out, and they stay tired!*

Great activity is not caused by great energy, but great activity produces great energy!

What you give is what you get, and what you get is what you give!

If you want the enthusiasm and energy of God in your life, give your life to Jesus Christ. Then you'll be in tune with an infinite cosmic source of unending, unlimited energy that will recycle itself as you do His happy work.

When I mentally plug into God's energy, I recharge my own!

Pray Right

"Now we rejoice in our wonderful new relationship with God—all because of what our Lord Jesus Christ has done in dying for our sins—making us friends of God."

Romans 5:11

You're not really alive unless you're enjoying enthusiasm and energy. God gave all of us basically the same equipment. Our glands, brains, shoulders, chests, hearts, blood vessel systems, and nervous systems are the same. There isn't much difference between bodies, but there is a great difference in our relationships with God. Some people keep a safe distance from the Lord and lead ho-hum lives; while others have a great relationship with Him, and through His Holy Spirit, God is stimulating and exciting them! They're alive!

Right now, if you've never accepted Jesus Christ into your life, your heart or your mind, do it! If you already have prayed this prayer, rededicate yourself!

Become an authentic Christian, then pray that the Holy Spirit will become a part of your life. If you do, you'll begin to discover great enthusiasm and energy for your life!

I believe the Holy Spirit is working in my life!

Pray Right

"And because you answer prayer, all mankind will come to you with their requests."

Psalm 65:2

At the end of every day, the last thing I do is pray, "Father in Heaven, Jesus Christ, I've sinned again today." I recall all the specific sins and confess them. Then I ask God to forgive me. And I know he does. He died on the cross for me . . . and for *you*. And on the strength of His promise and power to forgive sins, I can put my head on my pillow every night without any tinge of guilt! I've asked for forgiveness, and I know He gives it!

Then I pray for His Holy Spirit to fill my life. And I know he does. So, I sleep like a baby.

If I wake up very, very early it's because I'm so enthused and excited about what I can do for God that I can't wait to get dressed and get to work. And I begin each new day with this prayer: "Father, it's a brand new life. This new morning is a brand new day! Filled with bright new opportunities! Thank You for being a part of my life." Isn't that exciting?

Through prayer, Jesus is changing me!

Pray Right

"Always keep on praying. No matter what happens, always be thankful, for this is God's will for you who belong to Christ Jesus."
I Thessalonians 5:17,18

At the close of a meeting, I invited people to make a commitment to Jesus. I said, "If there's someone here who hasn't accepted Christ and you want to, while we're praying, lift your hand up, and with one finger pointing to Christ, say, 'Jesus, I want You in my life.'" As soon as I started to pray, a hand went up in the back of the auditorium. At the close of the service, a handsome young salesman in his 30's came up to me; and with tears in his eyes and his face radiating joy, he told me his story: He hadn't been to a church in twelve years, and then only for the funeral of his dad. He had never been a Christian and was living the way most worldly people do. He said, "Now suddenly I have the strange feeling I've been saved. Do you know what I mean!" I smiled and said, "You'd better believe I know what you mean!"

Jesus Christ was that for all of us! He wants to . . .

. . . release you from anything that would keep your enthusiasm from breaking out!

. . . reveal to you the possibilities for joyful and abundant living!

. . . give you the assurance that He's your friend in this life, and in the next one where you'll spend eternity with God!

**Jesus is the hero of my soul.
I love to talk with Him in prayer!**

Pray Right

*"You can get anything—**anything** you ask for in prayer—if you believe."*

Matthew 21:20

Dr. Norman Vincent Peale tells the story of a surgeon who talked about the most exciting surgery he performed . . . on a little girl with only a ten percent chance of survival.

"She was a tiny little thing under the sheet, ashen grey face, so frail, so weak and helpless. Just as the nurses were going to prepare her for anesthesia, she looked at me and said, 'Every night before I go to sleep I pray. May I pray a prayer now?' At that time I was having troubles of my own with my son and in my home, and I had become a very unhappy person. So I answered her, 'Sure, honey, and pray for your doctor, too.' Then she prayed, 'Jesus, tender Shepherd, hear me. Watch your little lamb tonight. Through the darkness be Thou near me, keep me safe 'til morning light. And Jesus, bless the doctor, because he's got troubles, too.'

It just broke me up. Embarrassed, I turned away from the others and pretended to wash up again so I could control myself and get rid of the tears. "O God," I prayed, "in my whole life if you ever use me to save a life, use me now to save this little girl!" The surgery was a success! Her life was saved! I felt as if I had been the one operated on that morning! Jesus had been put into me!"

The power of prayer is enriching my life!

LOOK TO THE MANGER TO FIND GOD'S GIFTS FOR YOU

The Gift of Faith

"But to all who received him, who believed in his name, he gave power to become children of God."
John 1:12

During a World Psychiatric Congress in Madrid, at the closing session on "Human Values in Psychotherapy," three lecturers spoke to over 4,000 psychiatrists and a few clergymen like myself.

The first one's opinion was that faith was vital. He said, "Build faith into your patients. Faith is a healing power."

The second lecturer spoke in German and contended that hope was the necessary ingredient. "Build hope into people, for hope is a saving power."

The last viewpoint was expressed by a speaker from Peru, "Give love to people. Non-judgmental, unselective, unconditional love. Only we psychiatrists can love unconditionally, because we alone are uncommitted to a moral or ideological value system. Therefore, we are not offended, and can truly love."

There has never been a person in human history who, more than Jesus Christ, came to symbolize the incarnation of faith, hope and love!

**Lord, help my seed of faith to grow
to maturity and bloom!**

The Gift of Faith

"For because of our faith, He has brought us into this place of highest privilege where we now stand, and we confidently and joyfully look forward to actually becoming all that God has had in mind for us to be."

Romans 5:2

A member of the Hour of Power congregation in New York City shared her story:

"I was in the hospital, very seriously ill, not expecting to live, and I tuned into your telecast. I met Jesus Christ, and I decided to choose faith."

"About the time the program was over, my doctor came into the room and I asked him, 'Do you think I'm going to live?' He looked at me and finally said, 'That's the wrong question. The right question is, do *you* think you're going to live?'"

"I put that together with what I had just heard on the television. You had said, 'Faith is believing what you cannot see. And the reward of faith is seeing what you have believed."

"Faith changed everything in my life. I chose to believe and I became well!"

Jesus Christ, thank you for believing in me even when it seems I'm not believing in You!

The Gift of Faith

"Faith is the confident assurance that something we want is going to happen. It is the certainty that what we hope for is waiting for us, even though we cannot see it up ahead."

Hebrews 11:1

Faith changes everything. You can believe Jesus Christ because He builds you up! People who sincerely and honestly seek to bring out the best within you are the ones to trust, and Jesus Christ is that kind of person.

He sees great possibilities in the most sinful human beings. He looked at Peter with all his faults, weaknesses, and sins and said, "I see you as a rock, and I'll build a church on you." He had faith in the good within people. He caused them to believe in themselves. And He planted the seeds of faith.

A psychologist once said, "Ultimately, I am not what I think I am. Nor am I what you think I am. I am what I think you think I am." We tend to fulfill the expectations that others have of us. So, look to Jesus because He thinks you're wonderful! He knows you have great possibilities!

**With Christ's faith in me,
I can dare to do great things!**

The Gift of Love

"God showed how much he loved us by sending his only Son into this wicked world to bring to us eternal life through his death."

I John 4:9

Some people feel that all religions are the same. But, that's not true. Christianity is distinctive in one sense. God, Who created the world and masterminded the universe, has incarnated Himself, has come down in human flesh.

I visited a friend in San Lucas, Mexico. Crawling around the bottom of his pool was a worm, ten inches long and as thick as my little finger. I said, "There's an illustration of why we need Christians." He didn't understand what I meant, so I explained that the worm didn't have the foggiest notion where it was. He didn't realize he was in Mexico, on planet earth, and part of a greater galaxy. Nor did he realize we were looking down watching him.

Human beings also have no awareness of God, Whose intelligence is so far superior to ours as ours is superior to that worm. If we wanted to communicate with that worm, we would have to become a worm.

God wanted to communicate with us, and He came down to tell us the truth. He did this in Jesus Christ!

My roots run deep into the positive stream of God's love.

The Gift of Love

"Love each other with brotherly affection and take delight in honoring each other."
                                                    Romans 12:10

I had an insight into a rare, precious, incredible, beautiful *impossibility!* (I don't use that word often.) What we all need is an experience of genuine love. But when you experience it, it is *impossible* to keep it! When you receive God's love into your life, you just have to give it away. That's the genius of Christmas!

Christians have the gift of love. That doesn't mean they're perfect, but they do have an emotional, spiritual cord that connects their immortal souls to the living Christ. He fills you with an unceasing compulsion to compassion. And in our human frailties when we do not express love, we are unhappy.

A non-Christian may feel good when he releases his hostilities and becomes angry. He finds delight and fulfillment in anger and temper. A Christian may be angry and vent his frustration, but it makes him miserable when he does. The gift of love will make you basically positive instead of negative. When you receive the gift of Christ's love, it will be impossible to keep. You'll give it away.

The experience of love is helping me experience more of today!

The Gift of Love

"And whatever you do, do it with kindness and love."

I am not immune to frustration. I learned a tremendous lesson a couple of years ago. I was upset, frustrated, furious! And I vented this in the presence of my wife. She really got to me when she said, "Bob, do you realize you're getting older?" I said, "Well, I suppose we all do get older, don't we?" She continued, "Have you observed old men?" I replied, "What in the world are you getting at?" She said, "I've observed old men and I notice they are either cuddly and twinkling like Santa Claus, cheerful, kind, nice old fellas; or they're crachety and crabby. Bob, as you get older, I hope you get more cuddly and twinkling, not crachety and crabby."

Christians aren't perfect, but they do have a direct connection with Jesus Christ. In this process His love flows in and controls us. Then we become more kind and loving. And as we become older, we become more beautiful, more cuddly and more twinkling.

**I feel the power of God's love
active within me!**

The Gift of Love

"For I have taken your lovingkindness and your truth as my ideals."
                                              Psalm 26:3

One man who works in our ministry came to a Christmas party at our home. I said, "Merry Christmas," to him as he entered, but he didn't respond. Someone noticed a look of dismay on my face and told me that he was really a wonderful guy. But he was deaf. And he was unable to talk. He works in the warehouse and doesn't have to talk to anybody. But he knows his job.

During the party I walked up to him and slowly asked if he read lips. He nodded yes. I said, "Merry Christmas!" And he mouthed, "Merry Christmas!"

Someone in our organization hired him. They told me he was unemployed and nobody would hire him. But our people did. Because Christians believe the best of people, and that's another way to express Christ's love.

**Today I will believe the best
about those I meet!**

The Gift of Love

"Lord, how I love you, for you have done such tremendous things for me."

Psalm 18:1

An employee in our ministry is a woman who works in the Prison Ministries. They collected 6,000 dozen cookies to give to the Chino Prison at Christmas. That's 72,000 homemade cookies! And all of them go to prisoners. Someone called me to say he thought it was terrible to collect money to make cookies for prisoners after they ripped us off. He believed in law and order, but he felt that prisoners deserved a lot more than they were getting. "We're too soft on these crooks," he said. My answer was simple, "They're not always going to be prisoners. They'll be coming out one of these days as better or worse people, and we're working to make them better!"

Our employee herself was a former prisoner. She became a Christian as a result of listening to Hour of Power, and decided when she got out she would help with the prison ministry. Somebody hired her because Christians believe the best about people.

God didn't believe any human being was useless. When He came down in Jesus Christ, He communicated that He believes in you! Christians receive God's love and can't help sharing it with others!

Lord, I appreciate your mercy, gentleness, and forgiveness!

The Gift of Love

"Be kind to each other, tenderhearted, forgiving one another, just as God has forgiven you because you belong to Christ."

Ephesians 4:32

Many years ago, my son and I built a little mountain cabin on a remote piece of property in the mountains. It took us a couple of years to finish. We finally saved enough money to fix it up, and we had a television, radio, stereo, fishing and skiing equipment ready for our retreats. One weekend we arrived to find everything had been stolen.

About two years later, the young man who had robbed us saw me in a store, approached me and asked for forgiveness. He told me he had been in jail, heard Hour of Power and accepted Christ!

When Christ enters your life, you have a connection to the Source of Love that will never let you go. You'll experience salvation and forgiveness of sins. And you'll never be able to keep it; you'll have to give it away.

**My heart is overflowing
with love and forgiveness!**

The Gift of Love

"And we know that all that happens to us is working for our good if we love God and are called according to His plans."

Romans 8:28

Every year we hear the words, "Christmas is for children." But I believe everybody needs Christmas, because everybody needs love!

Christmas is the time we remember that God gave us what we really wanted—genuine love. Jesus Christ went to the scum of the earth. He believed they were going to become the salt of the earth and the light of the world. He told them they were fishers of men and leaders of a great international movement of love and brotherhood. And, wow! They ended up believing it, because He believed it!

God loves you deeply, unconditionally, and eternally; and His gift of Jesus Christ is living proof!

Love is lifting the weights off me and giving me wings! I am free to love and be loved!

The Gift of Joy

"The fruit of the Spirit is love, joy, peace."
Galatians 5:22

If there was only one Christmas gift you could ask for this year and be assured that you would receive it, what would it be? For the person with terminal cancer, the obvious request would be healing. Someone with deep financial problems would probably ask for money. Another might ask for fame or power. Yet what do you really want more than any of these? *More than anything else, you want the gift of joy!*

I know wealthy people who have deliberaately become alcoholics because they can't cope with life. I know others in perfect health who wrestle with suicidal thoughts. You can have health, wealth, and fame, but if you lack joy, everything is nothing. Ultimately what you need is joy!

I am filled with the joy of the Lord now!

The Gift of Joy

*"But make everyone rejoice who puts his trust in
you. Keep them shouting for joy because you are
defending them. Fill all who love you with your
happiness."*

Psalm 5:11

First of all, joy is not the absence of tension. I
don't think there are any families happier than
ours, but we have had our share of tensions. With
five children, and four grandchildren, it's only
natural to have some conflicts.

I recall the sibling rivalry that has gone on in
our home. Especially how my son Bob used to
tease his sisters. He's an ordained minister now,
and one day I reminded him of an incident which
he had completely forgotten about. His little sister
had just started first grade and wanted badly to
say the prayer at the family dinner table. Bob said,
"You can't pray as good as I can." His sister
retorted, "I can, too. I learned a new prayer today
at school." So Bob said, "Okay, go ahead." And
she said, "I pledge allegiance to the flag, of the
United States of America . . ." No need to say this
caused quite a stir at our table.

Our home has not been free of tensions, yet it
is filled with joy!

I can experience joy even when I'm tense!

The Gift of Joy

"You have let me experience the joys of life and the exquisite pleasures of your own eternal presence."

Psalm 16:11

Nor is joy the absence of sorrow. If this seems like a grand paradox, it is. As a pastor for over thirty years, I have conducted a lot of funerals. In many of these, I have seen people weep. Yet through their sorrow, there was joy! Many people have wept bucketsful of tears, tears of gratitude for the years of love and joy they experienced. Parting is such sweet sorrow. There can be great joy in sadness, because joy is not the opposite of sorrow.

Joy is another word for love. Joy is the positive emotion that a human being experiences when he is really touched by God. When you have a tremendous spiritually positive feeling, it is joy—God's gift to you!

I can experience joy even in sorrow!

The Gift of Joy

"Our hearts ache, but at the same time we have the joy of the Lord. We are poor, but we give rich spiritual gifts to others. We own nothing, and yet we enjoy everything."

II Corinthians 6:10

How does God give joy? He does it by giving three gifts—salvation, self-esteem and service. I call these gifts a holy trinity. Some people get confused when Christians talk about the doctrine of the Holy Trinity. They can't believe there is one God but three persons.

The easiest way to explain the Holy Trinity is to talk about myself. I am one being named Robert Schuller, yet I am really three persons: Robert Schuller the body, Robert Schuller the brain, and Robert Schuller the heart. I am body, mind, and emotions, but I am one human being. Each separate part of me makes me who I am.

You can feel and probably have felt the trinity at work in you.

Pray today for new insight into the marvel that is your very own personal relationship with God.

I am filled with joy when I think of how good God is to me!

The Gift of Joy

"I bring you good tidings of great joy. For there is born to you this day in the city of David a Savior who is Christ the Lord."

Luke 2:10

So I am Robert Schuller, one but three persons. In the same way, God is three Persons in one God. God the Father is the mind, the Creator, and Architect of the universe. He is the God detached in the cosmic sense of space and time.

But God would not be a loving God if He never allowed us to see Him and touch Him. Therefore, He became human through the Incarnation. God took on a body through Jesus Christ.

If God were only a brain and body, He still would not be complete. So the Holy Spirit is God's heart. He is the emotional force, the vibrations God sends out to steer us towards Him.

You know that God is with you. So just as there is one God, made of God the Father, the Son and the Holy Spirit, there is a holy trinity within the gift of joy that God is giving to you.

The joy of the Lord is my strength!

The Gift of Joy

"Yet I will rejoice in the Lord; I will be happy in the God of my salvation."
Habakkuk 3:18

Salvation is to be forgiven of your sins, and to know your guilt is gone. It is the freedom to be able to put your head on the pillow at night and know when you waken, God will be walking with you into a new day. If you do not waken, you know God will be at the gates of heaven waiting for you. Salvation is God's gift to you when you receive Jesus Christ as your Savior.

Salvation accepted leads to self-esteem. If you know you are forgiven for your sins, and God is your Father and Friend, then you have a tremendous sense of self respect. You know you are a beautiful person. When God became human through the birth of Jesus Christ, it was His way of saying human beings are fantastic!

Salvation and self-esteem are mine through Jesus Christ!

The Gift of Joy

"But the angel reassured them. 'Don't be afraid!' he said. 'I bring the most joyful news ever announced, and it is for everyone! The Savior— yes, the Messiah, the Lord—has been born tonight in Bethlehem!'"

Luke 2:10,11

When God gives you salvation and self-esteem, He leads you into the third gift of joy—service.

A charter member of our church, Claire Landrus, wrote me about her mother, Kathryn Grant, who died at the age of 92. Mrs. Grant lived as a shut-in for the last eight years in the small town of Clarkston, Washington. As a shut-in, Mrs. Grant had a unique ministry. When people came to visit her, she would give *them* a lift. Claire's mother kept a diary and recorded her daily events. In the last ten months, Mrs. Grant had a total of 357 visits by 81 different people. Those who visited her left feeling better. One person summed it up to Claire, "Your mother put a bloom on so many days for so many people."

Anybody can be a servant of God. Whether you are shut-in, in a hospital bed, or active at work, you can know the salvation of Jesus Christ. You can receive the gifts of salvation, self-esteem and service—and experience real joy!

**Salvation, self-esteem and service
lead to real joy!**

The Gift of Peace

"Peace on earth. Goodwill to all."

Luke 2:14

One of the sweetest sentences in the Bible is today's Scripture. And yet skeptics and cynics say, "But there have been wars and rumors of wars since Jesus Christ came into the world. Not a few of them originated in countries that call themselves Christian. What do you make of that?" Jesus Himself said that there would be wars and rumors of wars until the end. So the questions arise: Did the angels make a mistake? Were they wrong? How are we to interpret what they said? To answer is simple. Peace came to this earth in Jesus Christ—the personal peace of soul that a human being can experience.

Do you have peace of soul? If not, do you know how to attain it?

You may have money, fame, academic credentials and power in business or politics, but without peace of soul, the rest is not worth it!

Fill my life, Lord, with your peace!

The Gift of Peace

"Let the peace of heart which comes from Christ be always present in your hearts and lives, for this is your responsibility and privilege as members of his body. And always be thankful."
Colossians 3:15

A professor, who was so learned he could teach biology, history, or astronomy, decided to motivate one of his young students by an all-day canoe trip in the wilderness. As they drifted downriver, a leaf fell into the canoe. "What kind of leaf is this?" asked the professor. The boy didn't know. "If you do not learn biology, you'll miss at least 20% of life's potential joy," said the wise old man.

"Do you know what Indians made those markings on the rocks?" The boy did not. "If you do not learn history, you'll miss another 20% of life's enjoyment," said the instructor. When darkness fell, he pointed to a constellation and asked, "What star is that?" The boy didn't know. "If you do not understand biology, history and astronomy, you'll miss a very large percentage of life."

Suddenly they heard a loud roar and realized their canoe was rapidly being carried along by swift current. The student asked, "Do you know how to swim?" The old man said, "no." As the boy dove into the river and swam to shore, he yelled back, "Then you're missing out on 100% of life." If you do not have peace of soul, you're missing it all.

Lord, my heart is flooded with the calm assurance of your presence!

The Gift of Peace

"May God our Father and the Lord Jesus Christ mightily bless each one of you, and give you peace."

II Corinthians 1:2

Peace of soul is not the absence of tension. God builds tension into life. It's part of life to keep us awake, to keep us challenged. Peace of soul is not the absence of insecurity. Change is constant and always produces some insecurities and tension.

The United States has experienced a lot of changes in the past few years. A change in administration doesn't necessarily imply there will be no tension. America is going to experience many difficulties in adjustment to change—which will move us all toward new growth!

America has problems. Economic problems are tied into productivity in an industrial world. And our productivity is down.

The history of economics proves that productivity actually creates more jobs. The jobs created are new, difficult and motivate us to learn new skills.

Therefore, peace of soul is not the absence of tension, insecurity, or economic stability. It's an experience that comes when your consciousness is expanded to comprehend the reality of God.

I am centered in the reality of my peace-giving Lord!

The Gift of Peace

"I am leaving you with a gift—peace of mind and heart! And the peace I give isn't fragile like the peace the world gives. So don't be troubled or afraid."

John 14:27

To comprehend the reality of God. God, who created the universe. God, who showed his face. That's what Christmas is all about!

Somehow a god who doesn't show himself in some way, wouldn't be a good god. He would be playing hide and seek, and game-playing would hurt his people.

But God made His presence felt in Jesus Christ. The message of God, who, through Christ gives peace of soul, is simple. He made Himself known for providence and pardon. God made it clear to us that as we trust Him and have faith in Him, He will help us through the rough times of life.

Peace of soul or peace of mind is the awareness that when something happens to us that is tragic, God can and will turn it into a triumph!

God's peace is not like the fragile peace of the world. It is durable and everlasting!

The Gift of Peace

"'Peace! Be still!' And the wind ceased, and there was a great calm."

Mark 4:39

On one of my speaking trips, a young couple with a baby approached me. They told me how Hour of Power helped them through a terribly difficult time. The young man said, "Three years ago my wife was killed in a tragic car accident." Then the young woman said, "And just thirty days later, my husband was driving at night and was killed in an accident." In unison they said, "God introduced us to each other." As they looked lovingly at each other they said, "Now we're married, and it's beautiful! Thank you for Hour of Power. It gives us hope." And then the husband made this classic statement, "God patched up the holes!"

God doesn't keep us from being torn, hurt, bleeding or crying. But Jesus came to this earth to tell us that God loves us and will patch up the holes. Peace of soul comes from a relationship with God where you treat Him when dark times come.

Nothing can distrub my sencse of peace!

The Gift of Peace

"I have said this to you, that in me you may have peace. In the world you have tribulation; but be of good cheer, I have overcome the world."
                                        John 16:33

Jesus Christ gives peace of soul by assuring salvation, pardon of all guilt and forgiveness of sins. You can handle anything when you know you have God as a close friend who loves you and cares about you. That's peace of soul!

I want to share the following part of a counseling session which took place here in our church office between a psychiatrist and a patient:

Doctor: "Do you see Jesus as Somebody who could love you?" Patient: "Yes." Doctor: "Somebody who can love you regardless of who you are, where you've been, or what you've done?" Tearfully, she replied, "If that were possible, what freedom it would give me." A long pause, then she said, "I think He wants to love me." Doctor: "Do you resist it?" Patient: "Yes. But why do I fight the very thing I want?" Doctor: "Perhaps you feel unworthy." She nodded affirmatively. Doctor: "That's the very meaning of the cross. Jesus was born to die. That's how much you're worth to God. God thinks you're worth the life of His Son!"

**Peace fills my heart and mind
for I know that God is with me!**

The Gift of Peace

"I'm sure you have heard about the Good News for the people of Israel—that there is peace with God through Jesus, the Messiah, who is Lord of all creation."

Acts 10:36

Jesus was born to die on a cross. His death, however, was not an execution by either the Romans or the Jews. Nor was it a suicide. It was a sacrifice by God for all people for all time. It was the forgiveness of sins.

Because of the crucifixion of Christ, you can go to Him and ask, "Jesus, are you hearing me?" Wait and hear in your mind the words, "Yes, I hear you." "Dear Jesus, did You die for me?" Hear this voice, "Yes, I did." Ask then, "Christ, will you be my Savior?" Listen to Him say, "Yes, I will because I love you."

Feel His arms embrace you and give you the peace of soul that makes life beautiful. Suddenly, the Christmas message of the angels will be real! It's happened to millions of people around the world, and it can happen to you! Come to your Savior today and receive the gift of Christmas peace!

**God's deep love for me produces
such inner peace!**

The Gift of Hope

"For unto us a Child is born; unto us a Son is given."

Isaiah 9:6

Christmas confirms that beautiful dreams can come true! God's beautiful dream for the world is people who through the Spirit of Jesus Christ begin to love each other and live together in peace.

It's possible—for you to have a better life. It's possible for dreams to come true!

What drives me and this ministry is the very deep awareness that we are all one family. And that's the way God looked at it on Christmas. He wasn't thinking in terms of just the Jewish people, His chosen people. If he came back today, it wouldn't be just for the United States of America, but for Christians everywhere! The Christmas message applies to everyone.

God offers you a Christmas gift today. It's two priceless words: IT'S POSSIBLE! It's possible there is a God Who knows you, loves you, and would die on a cross for you. It's not only possible, it's true!

Thank you, Jesus, for the hope that was born on Christmas!

The Gift of Hope

*"By his great mercy we have been born anew to
a living hope through the resurrection of Jesus
Christ from the dead."*

I Peter 1:3

During a staff meeting I told a story of an oceanliner
with several levels including the captain on top and
various other levels containing cabins, sundecks,
restaurants, a lounge, theater, engine room and, on
the bottom level, a washroom containing automatic
washers and dryers available for the passengers.

The little man who ran the washroom received no
attention from the passengers or crew. No one even
followed the rules in his washroom. He was getting fed
up with all the tourists taking towels, so he nailed them
to the outer wall of the ship. He never saw the
blueprints or plans of the ship, and he did not realize
that he had used an outer wall. But suddenly water
was leaking in—first slowly, then faster until it was up
to his ankles. He attempted to close up the holes to
no avail.

The point is *a hole in a boat is a hole in a boat.* All
human beings on planet earth are on the same ship.
And I'm very conscious of that. If you're hurting, I hurt,
If you have a problem, I have a problem. If you have
needs, I care about them because we're all in the same
boat. But the hope that was born on Christmas morn
bonded us together in such a positive way that
problems truly become possibilities!

**I choose to hope in God,
and I feel His presence!**

The Gift of Hope

"For with God, nothing is impossible."
Matthew 17:20

It's possible God has a plan for your life!

It's possible your life is called to have meaning and purpose more than you'll ever know.

It's possible that you might be forgiven all your sins, and saved from the hell of guilt.

It's possible that you'll be able to look at yourself in a mirror and feel proud yet completely humble at the same time!

It's possible that if you are discouraged, depressed or lacking in enthusiasm or zest for life that a new life can be yours!

Jesus Christ is the hope of the world, and with Him all things are possible!

Jesus Christ is the hope of the world!

The Gift of Hope

"Be joyful in hope."

Romans 12:12

From our church pulpit, a young man told how he decided to end his life on one particular Saturday night. He got a rifle, put the muzzle in his mouth and tried to pull the trigger with his big toe. The drinks he had consumed suddenly hit him and he passed out. He woke up the next morning to find that he hadn't pulled the trigger. He was alive!

The telephone rang. His attorney and friend called to invite him to church. They sat near the front and this young man heard every word the minister said. He cried all through the service. That day faith was born. Hope was born! And he began to believe that it's possible to have a beautiful life!

I am filled with joyful hope.
Life is exciting!

The Gift of Hope

"But blessed is the one who trusts in the Lord and has made the Lord his or her hope and confidence."
                                        Jeremiah 17:7

Three wisemen were told to "follow a star." I believe we should each follow a star. There is a star in your sky. If you can't see it, it's probably because clouds of disappointments, rejections, failures, hurts and setbacks cover it over. Don't say, "But I don't have the education. I don't have the connections. I don't belong to the right race. I don't belong to the right family. I'm not the right graduate of the right university. I don't have the money." Don't allow these thoughts to cloud your mind from the star. Never follow the clouds. Always follow the stars. Stars are permanent and clouds are not. Never hitch your wagon to a cloud, always to a star.

Believe in your dream, not your fears. Believe in your hopes, not your worries. Believe in your God-inspired goals, not your so-called impossible problems.

**Today I will concentrate on my hopes!
I'm worry-free!**

The Gift of Hope

"And so, Lord, my only hope is in you."
Psalm 39:7

Think of it—those wisemen followed a star! Do you suppose they solved the problems before they made the commitment? Could they be sure they'd find water along the road?

I have never travelled that way on land, but I have flown over the great desert all the way to Damascus. I couldn't help but think of those three wisemen who followed the same route, not by jet airplane with stewardesses, assuring them of water to drink and food to eat; not in an airplane which would take only a few hours and give them protection from the fatal killing sandstorms below that come as if by whim and without warning. They went on camels with very limited supplies. That's faith! That's love! That's hope! And they had the inspiration of a star!

It's still true that it's possible—for your life to have meaning, fulfillment, excitement and joy if you will find a star and follow it.

"And so, Lord, my only hope is in You."

The Gift of Hope

"Why be discouraged and sad? Hope in God!"
                                        Psalm 42:5

A prominent psychiatrist said, "All of us have had patients who sat in our offices, week after week, month after month, depressed, lifeless, dull, emotionally sick with skin sagging, eyes drooping, glassy and dull.

"Then came that moment in one of our counseling sessions when everything changed. We can't recall saying anything profound, and probably didn't, but we will never forget when the change took place.

"Suddenly the lifeless eyes come alive. The drooping eyelids open wide and the sparkle of life returns. The whole person is suddenly alive and alert to life! Why? Because hope has returned. And what is hope? How can we as doctors define this emotion, where it comes from and what it does to a person? We can only call it a human phenomenon."

The powerful spirit of hope that can change a person so dramatically is God! Hope is God's Spirit coming into a person to change his life and perspective! *Where there is hope, there is life!*

**I will be a messenger of hope
to someone else today!**